In the Beginning

Also by Donald Schmidt

God's Paintbrush Celebration Kit
(with Rabbi Sandy Eisenberg Sasso)

Emerging Word: a Creation Spirituality Lectionary

Bible Wonderings: Familiar Tales Retold

In the Beginning

✦

Creation Spirituality for the Days of Advent

Donald Schmidt

iUniverse, Inc.
New York Lincoln Shanghai

In the Beginning
Creation Spirituality for the Days of Advent

Copyright © 2007 by Donald Schmidt

iUniverse books may be ordered through booksellers or by contacting:

iUniverse
2021 Pine Lake Road, Suite 100
Lincoln, NE 68512
www.iuniverse.com
1-800-Authors (1-800-288-4677)

Because of the dynamic nature of the Internet, any Web addresses or links contained in this book may have changed since publication and may no longer be valid.

ISBN: 978-0-595-44812-8 (pbk)
ISBN: 978-0-595-89131-3 (ebk)

Printed in the United States of America

All artwork by Fred Lorenzo, Lahaina, Maui, Hawai'i.
The cover illustration is from an original 14" x 18" watercolor, *The Beginning.*
Image on p. 1 is from an original 16" x 16" watercolor, *Ohana.*
Image on p. 33 is from an original 14" x 18" watercolor, *Searching.*
Image on p. 63 is from an original 14" x 14" watercolor, *Honu Abstract.*
Image on p. 89 is from an original 18" x 24" watercolor, *A Little Love.*
Limited edition, full color giclée prints of these images are available from Lorenzo Studios, 677 Luakini St., Lahaina, HI, 96761. Telephone 808-205-2363.

For Louie, Rita, Sarah, and Eric—
you embody hope, and new beginnings.

And for Don, just because ...

Contents

Introduction

You don't have to use this book in Advent. I know, the title implies that you should, and several of the themes connect quite clearly with that season. But you really can use it any time. You don't have to use it as a book of daily reflections, either—although that's how it's designed.

In the Beginning is a simple journey through the four paths of Creation Spirituality, taken over four weeks. However, given that there are four paths, and four weeks in the season of Advent, it seemed logical to put them together.

If you are not familiar with Creation Spirituality, I have provided the briefest of introductions in the Appendix—it's called "The Magi and the Spiritual Journey" and it introduces the four paths in the context of Matthew 2:1-12. For a more in depth introduction, I would refer you to a couple of books by Matthew Fox, either *Original Blessing* (published by Jeremy Tarcher/Putnam) or *Creation Spirituality: Liberating Gifts for the Peoples of the Earth* (published by Harper San Francisco). Both are good, although *Original Blessing* has been around for almost 25 years and is an absolute classic.

How the book is set up

In the Beginning is designed to be read one section a day, leading up to Christmas. To this end, the pages are dated, beginning on November 27. Why that day? For the simple reason that I have provided seven readings for each week, and if you start on that day, you will conveniently arrive at December 25 right on schedule.

If you want to read the book differently, be my guest—just ignore the dates, or pencil in other ones. For example, if you are adamant about wanting to start on the First Sunday of Advent (such as December 2, 2007; November 30, 2008; November 29, 2009; or November 28, 2010) that's absolutely fine. You might want to double up a couple of dates, or figure out another way to make things fit. It's all up to you.

There's also a Prelude to read as you begin, and a Postlude for Christmas Day.

A study guide for group use is available at www.emerging word.com.

Bible translation

There are lots of English translations of the Bible, and each one has its good points and its not so good points. There are some great passages in every translation, and some that I'm less enthused about. Consequently, I struggled greatly with which translation to use—or even whether to include scripture texts at all.

But I thought, if you want to read this book while at the beach, atop a mountain, or riding on a bus, it would be convenient not to have to take a copy of the Bible along with you, so I decided to include the scripture readings for each day. I alternate between the *New Revised Standard Version* and *The Message*.

The Message is comfortable to read, and translator Eugene Peterson brings a freshness to the text that is exciting and challenging. However, being a paraphrase, sometimes it strays a little too far from the original text for my liking, and the language is not as inclusive as it could be.

On the other hand, the *New Revised Standard Version* is extremely accurate to the original manuscripts, and tends to be quite inclusive in its use of pronouns for people, but sometimes the English seems a bit stiff and lifeless.

Occasionally, I have quoted other translations, and used my own paraphrases, and most of all I would invite you—encourage you, in fact—to read the biblical texts in your own preferred translation. I have included them here simply for the sake of convenience.

The Season of Advent

It is a time of waiting, a time of wondering, a time of preparing.

Often we do that guided by words from the ancient prophets of Israel, setting us up with a sense of longing and, in some cases, almost a sense of prediction that Jesus is coming to fulfill a long-term plan of God's.

Yet maybe it can be something different.

For centuries, churches have used lectionaries—sets of scripture readings for each Sunday—to guide our spiritual journeys. The lectionary readings for Advent have often focused on that sense of longing, and hoping, and preparing. There is anything wrong with that.

But I like to wonder, and I like to approach things from various angles.

My doctoral dissertation at Wisdom University was to create a different kind of lectionary, one that was based on the four paths of Creation Spirituality. (The lectionary is available as a book called *Emerging Word*—see p. 137 for more information.)

For the Advent portion of that lectionary, I chose one path for each week, and this book of meditations follows that pattern.

The scriptures and the season invite us into a dance with the particular path being explored, and together we embark on a spiritual journey leading to the celebration of Christ's birth. Who knows where it will take us beyond there, but I am convinced it will take us somewhere exciting, somewhere challenging.

That's the point: not to land at Christmas, but to arrive there ready to be changed. Like the shepherds, we go to the stable not quite knowing what to expect, but we go away transformed, ready to live new lives, having encountered the Christ in the baby in the manger.

Come, let's see where Advent might lead us.

Prelude: Original Blessing

Genesis 1:1, *King James Version*
In the beginning God created the heaven and the earth.

> *Life is either a great adventure or nothing.*
> —*Helen Keller.*

In the beginning—in the very beginning—God.

Years ago, when the Apollo 8 astronauts first orbited the moon, they had the phenomenal experience of seeing an earth-rise: our entire planet, in the galactic distance, behind the moon.

The image appeared on a U.S. postage stamp, with the caption "In the beginning, God …"

Good words: In the beginning, God …

It's a bit of an oxymoron if you think about it. The text says "in the beginning" and then goes on to say that there was something before the beginning. Two somethings, actually: total chaos (formless void), and God. It's just that our comprehension of *beginning* really only goes back to *our* beginning. If not necessarily our human beginning, then at least our cosmic beginning. We don't have the capacity to comprehend the fact that there is no beginning. Because there was always God, and God didn't have a beginning. God always was, even before forever.

But for us, there is a beginning, and so we begin our journey—our human journey, our spiritual journey, our Advent journey—with a story of beginnings.

The story begins with the statement that God was there, at the outset, creating things. Creating things with words. More precisely, making sense out of things.

God speaks, and it is so. The formless void (I love the Hebrew word for this: *tohu v'vohu*—one of my university professors said the word is best translated "gobbledygook") begins to coalesce from nothingness into somethingness. Because God decreed it. Because God said, "let there be." That's all it took.

God's word has amazing power in this story. It sets the stage for more and more of what is to come. God's word throughout the biblical story is going to have even more amazing power. We'll see this as the gospel of John retells Genesis 1:1 with parallels to Jesus. God's word made flesh. But let's not get ahead of ourselves. Let's focus on the word back at the beginning.

Words take breath, and it is God's breath, God's spirit, that is hovering over the deep giving birth to creation in this story. God's breath, issuing forth in powerful, creative, life-giving word.

And it all makes sense. The author of this story wants to make that abundantly clear. There is a pattern, an order, to this universe. We may not understand it, but God does. God created it in a neat, coordinated way, so that things would work together in appropriate patterns, with harmony and balance. Not that these are rigid rules that the universe must follow, as testified by the uniqueness of each living thing, but rather that there is a way (a *torah,* in Hebrew) for everything to work together. It *can* work. There can be balance.

When life doesn't make sense to us, it still makes sense to God. And when it really doesn't make sense to us, and becomes overwhelming, maybe we need to take a little time out, and look again at the created "order." Get out of ourselves, and experience the universe—or at least some of it.

We notice the birds and flowers, the simple rhythms of day and night and seasons. Leaves seem to know when to fall, and water always knows to tumble downhill. Mountains stay up (most of the time) and oceans ebb and flow within their boundaries (most of the time). It seems the universe is saying to us, "Life isn't perfect, but it has a rhythm and a pattern, and it can make sense. Most of the time."

Now, I know that there are other explanations for how things work, explanations that are true and accurate and real. Explanations about a primal flaring forth billions of years ago that created all matter. I know and believe and affirm the understandings of science, cosmology, and evolution. To ignore those facts would be silly.

But just as silly would be to ignore this Genesis story, too. For, as a story, it tells us one way to understand God's place in all of this. Not *how* it happened, but what God intended in all of it.

This is the story of the origins of the universe.

This is the story of original blessing.

This is *our* story.

Week One:
the via positiva

Wetness is beauty:
ocean, rain, river, and spring—
all places of birth.

November 27

Genesis 1:1-2:4, *THE MESSAGE*

[1]First this: God created the Heavens and Earth—all you see, all you don't see. [2]Earth was a soup of nothingness, a bottomless emptiness, an inky blackness. God's Spirit brooded like a bird above the watery abyss.

[3]God spoke: "Light!"
    And light appeared.
[4]God saw that light was good
    and separated light from dark.
[5]God named the light Day,
    he named the dark Night.
It was evening, it was morning—
    Day One.
[6]God spoke: "Sky! In the middle of the waters;
    separate water from water!"
[7]God made sky.
    He separated the water under sky
from the water above sky.
    And there it was:
[8]he named sky the Heavens;
    It was evening, it was morning—
Day Two.
[9]God spoke: "Separate!
    Water-beneath-Heaven, gather into one place;
Land, appear!"
    And there it was.
[10]God named the land Earth.
    He named the pooled water Ocean.
    God saw that it was good.
[11]God spoke: "Earth, green up! Grow all varieties

of seed-bearing plants,
Every sort of fruit-bearing tree."
    And there it was.
[12]Earth produced green seed-bearing plants,
    all varieties,
And fruit-bearing trees of all sorts.
    God saw that it was good.
[13]It was evening, it was morning—
    Day Three.
[14]God spoke: "Lights! Come out!
    Shine in Heaven's sky!
Separate Day from Night.
    Mark seasons and days and years,
[15]Lights in Heaven's sky to give light to Earth."
    And there it was.
[16]God made two big lights, the larger
    to take charge of Day,
The smaller to be in charge of Night;
    and he made the stars.
[17]God placed them in the heavenly sky
    to light up Earth
[18]And oversee Day and Night,
    to separate light and dark.
    God saw that it was good.
[19]It was evening, it was morning—
    Day Four.
[20]God spoke: "Swarm, Ocean, with fish and all sea life!
    Birds, fly through the sky over Earth!"
[21]God created the huge whales,
    all the swarm of life in the waters,
And every kind and species of flying birds.
    God saw that it was good.
[22]God blessed them: "Prosper! Reproduce! Fill Ocean!

Birds, reproduce on Earth!"
²³It was evening, it was morning—
Day Five.
²⁴God spoke: "Earth, generate life! Every sort and kind:
cattle and reptiles and wild animals—all kinds."
²⁵And there it was:
wild animals of every kind,
Cattle of all kinds, every sort of reptile and bug.
God saw that it was good.
²⁶God spoke: "Let us make human beings in our image,
make them reflecting our nature
So they can be responsible for the fish in the sea,
the birds in the air, the cattle,
And, yes, Earth itself,
and every animal that moves on the face of Earth."
²⁷God created human beings;
he created them godlike,
Reflecting God's nature.
He created them male and female.
²⁸God blessed them:
"Prosper! Reproduce! Fill Earth! Take charge!
Be responsible for fish in the sea and birds in the air,
for every living thing that moves on the face of Earth."
²⁹Then God said, "I've given you
every sort of seed-bearing plant on Earth
And every kind of fruit-bearing tree,
given them to you for food.
³⁰To all animals and all birds,
everything that moves and breathes,
I give whatever grows out of the ground for food."
And there it was.
³¹God looked over everything he had made;
it was so good, so very good!

It was evening, it was morning—
   Day Six.
2:[1]Heaven and Earth were finished,
   down to the last detail.
[2]By the seventh day
   God had finished his work.
On the seventh day
   he rested from all his work.
[3]God blessed the seventh day.
   He made it a Holy Day
Because on that day he rested from his work,
   all the creating God had done.
[4]This is the story of how it all started,
   of Heaven and Earth when they were created.

God is the good and all things which proceed from him are good.
—Hildegard of Bingen

God creates by speaking, by uttering a divine word.

Yet another word deserves our attention in this passage, and I fear it too often gets missed. We might read it, and even hear it, but we do not embrace it.

Or perhaps we ignore it, or we assume it pertains to others, but not us.

The word is "good."

Good.

It's in there six times.

And the last time, it's proclaimed as "very good."

In our time and place this has become the most important word in the entire story, because it has been forgotten. Worse still, there are those who, perhaps out of a sense of guilt, came up with the non-biblical notion of original sin and used it as an eraser on this profound and precious text.

It is good.

God said it.

Did God not mean it?

Or are human beings somehow so incredibly powerful that we can render this statement null and void? I hope we don't presume ourselves so great and mighty that we can, in one fell swoop, declare God's miraculous and wondrous handiwork all bad.

If you think about it, the idea is pretty ridiculous. It defies the very core of this story, and it defies the power of God. So, before we move any further into the Bible or into Advent, let us ground ourselves firmly in this story.

It is good.

When my children were growing up we had a book called *The Family Story Bible.* Like many other young children, my girls wanted the same few stories read over and over and over again.

One of the favorites was the creation story. They loved the beautiful bright pictures of the garden and the animals. But the most fun thing of all was creating a little litany. Repeated in the story was the refrain, "And God said, 'that's good.'"

Each time I would get to that part, the girls would say "that's good" with great enthusiasm.

I imagine that God said it with that same, wonderful, child-like enthusiasm. God is not so much making a statement for the ages here as admiring divine creativity and proudly saying, "good!"

Good job, good stuff.

The creation is good.

The mountains and the trees and the pomegranates, the kangaroos and moose and rivers and tulips and sparrows, the sound of thunder and the silence of sunrise. Even the swamps. Even the uneven places.

It is good.

All of it.

Every last atom.

Perhaps the most amazing thing of all: God creates, for better or worse, something in God's image called human.

And upon creating that thing, God declares that they/we are "very good."

Can you believe it?

We should.

God says that we are very good.

There are times—as we will explore in the *via negativa*—when God gets frustrated with us, when things do not always go well, when we find ourselves distanced from God, when we *feel* bad. That's real. That's part of life. Lots of biblical writers will tell us that, and we can readily relate to them. Artists and poets and ordinary people throughout the ages have expressed how we often move away from God, and experience the consequences.

But feeling bad and being bad are not the same thing.

Doing bad things and being bad are not the same thing.

Treating God badly and being bad are not the same thing.

So much for original sin. It's original blessing, pure and simple. Deny it, argue it, try our hardest to wish it away, the truth is that's how the story begins. With God saying "it is good."

The rest of the story is about God wanting to restore a relationship with us that got broken early on. It's about God wanting us to get back to awareness of the good, awareness that we are God's creatures, loved by the one who made us and first called us good that warm, gentle day long, long, long ago.

So we begin the Advent season in the beginning, remembering we are created by God. And we go into this season not so much longing for redemption as eagerly awaiting breakthrough, and a new journey with Christ, the Word of God that called us into being, and said from day one "it is good."

November 28

Genesis 1:2 7-3 1, NRSV

²⁷So God created humankind in his image, in the image of God he created them; male and female he created them.

²⁸God blessed them, and God said to them, "Be fruitful and multiply, and fill the earth and subdue it; and have dominion over the fish of the sea and over the birds of the air and over every living thing that moves upon the earth."

²⁹God said, "See, I have given you every plant yielding seed that is upon the face of all the earth, and every tree with seed in its fruit; you shall have them for food. ³⁰And to every beast of the earth, and to every bird of the air, and to everything that creeps on the earth, everything that has the breath of life, I have given every green plant for food." And it was so.

³¹God saw everything that he had made, and indeed, it was very good. And there was evening and there was morning, the sixth day.

Forfeit awe and the world becomes a marketplace.
—Abraham Joshua Heschel

One of Gary Larson's *The Far Side* cartoons shows a lovely wilderness scene, and in the midst of it God has dropped a jar of humans. The jar has obviously broken, the humans have escaped, and from the heavens comes a cry of "uh-oh."

It's understandable.

Life changed when we came along.

Not necessarily for the better, not necessarily for the worse, but it changed.

That's why I thought it worth repeating this portion of Genesis 1, that we might focus a little more closely on the section where God creates the human beings, because there's a lot of stuff in there.

First of all, let's notice that we are creators.

We are artists, all of us.

How do we know this? Because we are created in the image of God, and God is nothing if not a creator. Certainly that's what's going on in the story so far.

We yearn to create, and yet sadly far too often the creative instinct gets thwarted. It gets laughed at. It gets put down.

Or we believe we don't have time to be creators. We have to do "real work" and our creativity has to take a back seat.

Or we do not recognize the creativity in the work we do. We do not value—or are not encouraged to value—what we produce, what we create.

How often have you heard someone say "I can't draw" or "I cannot dance" (perhaps you've said it yourself)? And yet we can, every one of us, for we are created in the image of God, the Creator. And whether we have the gifts of da Vinci or not, the tools of an art school or not, even whether we have hands or not, we can draw—on a canvas or in our minds. And we can dance, with our feet, our hands, our torsos, our hearts.

We *can* create, and we *do* create, and we must affirm our creation. For when we do that, we affirm our place and our value as people created in the image of God. And that, over and above anything else, is who we are.

We are created to "rule over" the other creatures in *Today's New International Version* or to have "dominion over" in the *New Revised Standard Version*. Oh, how that phrase has gotten us into trouble. I think it's because we let the power aspect of those words go to our heads, and we forget the "made in the image of God part."

We forget, I think, how God rules. This is where, frankly, I prefer the word *dominion* because it has the Latin root *dominus*. Usually that word gets translated as "Lord" and it has all sorts of hierarchical connotations, usually negative, for a lot of people.

But let's pause for a moment, and remember that we're in Advent, preparing for Christmas. We're preparing for the birth of Jesus, God incarnate, demonstrating ultimate power and sovereignty and presence by lying as a helpless baby in a manger.

There's a clue here.

This is "Lord-ship," God style.

This is how God "dominates."

This is how God rules. We have the Jesus model.

It would even be okay to say we are to "Lord it over" (not my favorite choice of words, but work with me here for a moment) creation, if we would only remember that the model God gives for how to do that is one of companion and compassion.

The act of ruling over the birds and fish and animals is not to stomp them into oblivion but to co-exist with them in harmony, finding ways to share the planet with them in a way that works for all of us—the balance thing. That's how God would do it. Kind of makes sense, doesn't it?

Even the Hebrew word *rada* that gets translated as *dominion* or *rule* here has a sense of care-giving or nurturing, such as a just, fair, and compassionate monarch might provide, rather than exploiting.

Perhaps some people let the power sense of the word "dominion" go to their heads because of the instruction to "subdue" the earth in verse 28. But the Hebrew here really means to subdue the earth in terms of tilling the soil. Again, makes sense in context. But we have tended to get a little carried away over the years.

In *The Message*, which was the version of this same passage in yesterday's reading, Eugene Peterson used words like

let us make human beings in our image,
reflecting our nature,
so they can be responsible ...
God created human beings;
he created them godlike.

That's what it is to have dominion: to be godlike. To reflect God's nature. To be responsible.

God created a world with wonderful balance—a system that could take care of itself, especially if managed lovingly and carefully by these beautiful creatures created in God's own image.

November 29

Genesis 2:4b-25, THE MESSAGE

At the time God made Earth and Heaven, [5]before any grasses or shrubs had sprouted from the ground—God hadn't yet sent rain on Earth, nor was there anyone around to work the ground [6](the whole Earth was watered by underground springs)—[7]God formed Man out of dirt from the ground and blew into his nostrils the breath of life. The Man came alive—a living soul!

[8]Then God planted a garden in Eden, in the east. He put the Man he had just made in it. [9]God made all kinds of trees grow from the ground, trees beautiful to look at and good to eat. The Tree-of-Life was in the middle of the garden, also the Tree-of-Knowledge-of-Good-and-Evil.

[10]A river flows out of Eden to water the garden and from there divides into four rivers. [11]The first is named Pishon; it flows through Havilah where there is gold. [12]The gold of this land is good. The land is also known for a sweet-scented resin and the onyx stone. [13]The second river is named Gihon; it flows through the land of Cush. [14]The third river is named Hiddekel and flows east of Assyria. The fourth river is the Euphrates.

[15]God took the Man and set him down in the Garden of Eden to work the ground and keep it in order.

[16]God commanded the Man, "You can eat from any tree in the garden, [17]except from the Tree-of-Knowledge-of-Good-and-Evil. Don't eat from it. The moment you eat from that tree, you're dead."

[18]God said, "It's not good for the Man to be alone; I'll make him a helper, a companion." [19]So God formed from the dirt of the ground all the animals of the field and all

the birds of the air. He brought them to the Man to see what he would name them. Whatever the Man called each living creature, that was its name. [20]The Man named the cattle, named the birds of the air, named the wild animals; but he didn't find a suitable companion.

[21]God put the Man into a deep sleep. As he slept he removed one of his ribs and replaced it with flesh. [22]God then used the rib that he had taken from the Man to make Woman and presented her to the Man.

[23]The Man said,

>   "Finally! Bone of my bone,
>   flesh of my flesh!
> Name her Woman
>   for she was made from Man."

[24]Therefore a man leaves his father and mother and embraces his wife. They become one flesh.

[25]The two of them, the Man and his Wife, were naked, but they felt no shame.

One of our chief jobs in life, it seems to me, is to realize how rare and valuable each one of us really is—that each of us have something which no one else has—or ever will have—something inside which is unique to all time.
—Fred Rogers

In Genesis 1, God spoke and worlds came into being. In Genesis 2, God takes more of a hands on approach—literally.

The Hebrew verb that gets used for God's activity is that of a potter, taking clay from the ground, and forming a human being from it. It is—pardon the pun—a very down to earth story. Where the image of God in the other story was as a stage director, here God is more intimately involved, dirtying divine hands and breathing divine breath into a handful of mud, that we might have life.

After God creates human life, God sets about creating things—living things like plants and rivers—but also things like rules ("don't eat from that tree").

God begins to create something else as well.

Professor W.J.A. Power once told this story to a group of children in a Sunday School class. At the end of it all, he asked the children what this story told them God must be like. One child said, "that story says that God likes us."

God likes us.

God looks upon the first human and thinks, "hmmm. Poor fellow's going to be lonely. This will never do. Let's see if we can work on that." And along come the giraffes and mice and sheep and koalas and cats and water buffalo, the eagle and parrot and sparrow. All lovely, but not quite what the doctor ordered.

It dawns on God that perhaps something else is needed. (And yes, it really does seem to dawn on God—there isn't any kind of recipe being followed here at all.)

So a second human being is created, and this is a crowning moment in the story. That the first one is male and the second one female has caused no end of difficulties over history, but to dwell on that I think causes us to miss the deeper point here.

When Power was talking to that Sunday School class, his final question to the children was, "What is it that the story says that a person needs?" And the child replied, "Someone to love and with whom to be a friend."[1]

That's the point, isn't it?

Someone with whom to be a friend.

Of all the marvelous insights this story gives us, it tells us that God cares about us enough to invent friendship, companionship, right off the bat. We are not destined to be alone in this world.

Now, I'll quickly tell you I'm an introvert and I like to crawl off and be by myself from time to time. Solitude is a wonderful thing. This passage does not say we all must be married, or hang about in crowds all the time, or anything like that. But it does tell us that God creates us to be in relationship with one another, to be community. To care for one another.

In John 15:15, Jesus spoke about friendship.

"I don't call you servants," he said, "I call you friends." As Jesus invited all kinds of people into the new community that he was forming, he redefined what it means to be family. Jesus modeled a new form of kinship, based on caring for one another, instead of being based on ties of biology or legal documents. Jesus reminded us that family, that friendships, that community are part of God's intention for humankind.

That's a key part of this Genesis story.

God didn't just create things in this story, God created something more.

Life.

And beyond that, relationships, and community.

Friendship.

Thanks be to God.

November 30

Proverbs 8:2 2-3 1, NRSV

22[Wisdom speaks:] The LORD created me at the beginning of his work,
    the first of his acts of long ago.
23Ages ago I was set up,
    at the first, before the beginning of the earth.
24When there were no depths I was brought forth,
    when there were no springs abounding with water.
25Before the mountains had been shaped,
    before the hills, I was brought forth—
26when he had not yet made earth and fields,
    or the world's first bits of soil.
27When he established the heavens, I was there,
    when he drew a circle on the face of the deep,
28when he made firm the skies above,
    when he established the fountains of the deep,
29when he assigned to the sea its limit,
    so that the waters might not transgress his command,
    when he marked out the foundations of the earth,
30then I was beside him, like a master worker;
    and I was daily his delight,
    rejoicing before him always,
31rejoicing in his inhabited world
    and delighting in the human race.

Bless those who play like children. May they infect all those who doubt.
—Hawksley Workman

In the beginning, God created.

We learned that when we read Genesis.

And we learned that what God created was good. All of it. That is the beauty and blessing of the *via positiva*.

But what did God create first?

Wisdom, according to Proverbs 8:22.

We know this because Wisdom herself *(Hochmah* in Hebrew, *Sophia* in Greek) tells us so.

But just who is Wisdom?

In both Hebrew and Greek, like many other languages, nouns can be either masculine or feminine. And in both of those languages, "wisdom" is a feminine noun. Thus, whenever Wisdom is personified, as in this text from Proverbs, or when Wisdom is identified with God, she is always portrayed as a woman.

She is more than just knowledge, more than just data. Wisdom is the stuff that you *know*, that you know by heart, that you know in your guts, in the depth of your being. The things that make you, well, wise, as opposed to the data that simply makes you smart. In a folksy way of putting it, it's common sense as opposed to book learning.

In the Hawaiian language, one speaks of the *na'au* (nah-ow), literally the intestines or the bowels, as the seat of both emotions and wisdom. In the same way that in English we would speak of "heart" or "mind," in Hawaiian one would refer to the *na'au*. The Hawaiian word for wisdom, interestingly, is *na'au'ao* (nah-ow-a-oh), or the things that emanate from both heart and mind—together, from the depth of the self.

So, we have Wisdom, the first thing created by God.

As some translations state it, Wisdom is the first thing present with God at the beginning of creation. That's an interesting way to put it if one sees Wisdom as an aspect of the Divine, and not a creation.

Still other translations refer to Wisdom as the first thing "brought forth" by God, which is interesting again, if one sees Wisdom as something "begotten, not made" which is how John will describe the Christ many centuries later. John will say that this same Christ is the Word that was with God in the beginning.

Great stuff to ponder during Advent.

Now, just what was Wisdom doing, in the beginning, with God?

She was creating.

She was playing.

You see, this text just overflows with ambiguity, which is great in a season already pregnant with wonder and multiple meanings.

In Proverbs 8:30, Wisdom is described with the Hebrew word *amon*, which can be translated in a couple of ways, either of which is perfectly legitimate. One of these is often rendered "master worker" or "artisan." This presents us with the image of God's assistant, side by side with God as co-creator, helping God to design and craft the universe in all its glory and splendor. I can almost imagine them consulting, laughing together.

"What do you think, is the giraffe's neck a little too long?"

"No, just right I think. After all, something has to eat the leaves at the top of the trees."

The rest of verses 30 and 31 speak thus of Wisdom delighting in God's presence, rejoicing in humankind and all that God was doing. Laughter! Joy! Blessing! Things are good, and God has someone with whom to share the joy of the creative act. What a delightful image.

Yet the other way of translating it—which is just as correct as the first—contains its own delightful imagery. This one reads "I was with God as a little child, delighting God in the act of creation."

Wisdom as a little child.

Now, have you ever tried to do a task with a toddler under foot? Even the simplest thing can become an intensely complicated ordeal, frustrating beyond recognition.

Yet, in the midst of all the frustration, a child's smile, giggle, or creative attempt at assistance can turn things into a wonderful joy. Or can cause us to see something in a new and intriguing way.

The Bible presents us here with a very illuminating image. A child present with God at the moment of the creation of the world.

No, I'm not reading this into the text—it's right there in the original.

A child, running around on the floor while God is in the act of whirling planets into space and trying to measure out the right amount of gravity to keep the mountains from toppling over, and establishing umpteen centuries' worth of tide tables. One glitch and who knows where we'd be. It boggles the mind.

It's beautiful.

It's amazing.

I don't know why the author placed this story here. But I know that when I read it, I move that much closer to God. I move that much closer to my Creator, remembering that I am created by a God who loves me and knows me with all of my funny little quirks.

Of course, I don't really think that the creation of the universe happened in any kind of setting where it was possible for a toddler literally to roam around on the floor. Or for there to have been a floor there in the first place. But I don't think for one nanosecond that that's the point here. There is—if I can risk a dreadful pun—a powerful wisdom (with a lowercase "w") in this story.

God doesn't want us to take the details of these stories nearly as seriously as the stories themselves. The stories tell us that God is behind the universe, behind the creation of it all, behind the logic of it all, behind the basics of it all. God is behind the blessing, the joy, the laughter, the relationships, the hopes, and the dreams.

That's the Wisdom of the thing.

December 1

Isaiah 40: 1-1 1, THE MESSAGE

[1]"Comfort, oh comfort my people,"
    says your God.
[2]"Speak softly and tenderly to Jerusalem,
    but also make it very clear
That she has served her sentence,
    that her sin is taken care of—forgiven!
She's been punished enough and more than enough,
    and now it's over and done with."
[3]Thunder in the desert!
    "Prepare for GOD's arrival!
Make the road straight and smooth,
    a highway fit for our God.
[4]Fill in the valleys,
    level off the hills,
Smooth out the ruts,
    clear out the rocks.
[5]Then GOD's bright glory will shine
    and everyone will see it.
    Yes. Just as GOD has said."
[6]A voice says, "Shout!"
    I said, "What shall I shout?"
"These people are nothing but grass,
    their love fragile as wildflowers.
[7]The grass withers, the wildflowers fade,
    if GOD so much as puffs on them.
    Aren't these people just so much grass?
[8]True, the grass withers and the wildflowers fade,
    but our God's Word stands firm and forever."
[9]Climb a high mountain, Zion.

You're the preacher of good news.
Raise your voice. Make it good and loud, Jerusalem.
You're the preacher of good news.
Speak loud and clear. Don't be timid!
Tell the cities of Judah,
"Look! Your God!"
[10]Look at him! GOD, the Master, comes in power,
ready to go into action.
He is going to pay back his enemies
and reward those who have loved him.
[11]Like a shepherd, he will care for his flock,
gathering the lambs in his arms,
Hugging them as he carries them,
leading the nursing ewes to good pasture.

Belief in God means trusting that a good Power is at work in our world and surrendering ourselves to It. So, in practice, belief in God is belief in life. It is to take things as they come and, always finding and furthering the good, to make the best of every situation. Thus, every person of goodwill, whether a believer or not, is actually involved in the same commitment.
—*Daniel A. Helminiak*

I recall my grandmother as being rather strict. Kind, in her own way, but strict. Perhaps raising seven children on a farm imposes a certain strictness on one, or maybe it was just the times.

In any event, as children we at times feared her. In particular, she had a reputation amongst the grandchildren for using a wooden spoon upon our backsides as a disciplinary measure.

Now, to be fair to her memory I have to say that I cannot, at this stage of my life, honestly recall her actually using the wooden spoon on me. But I very clearly, to this day, recall the potential threat of the thing.

One time we were visiting at Grandma's house and her wooden spoon broke—probably in the innocent act of stirring cake batter or perhaps bread dough.

The rejoicing amongst the grandchildren (well out of Grandma's earshot, mind you), was akin to the munchkins of Oz at the dropping of Dorothy's house.

But our joy was short-lived. Some time later, upon returning from the store, a tell-tale wooden handle could be seen protruding from the top of a shopping bag. In fear and dread, one of my cousins asked, "Grandma, did you buy another wooden spoon?"

"Comfort my people," God says. "Comfort them. Tell them their punishment is over."

Tell them they can come out of their room. Tell them that they can get out of the time-out chair, that they can come down to dinner, that they can have dessert after all.

Tell them that I have thrown away my wooden spoon.

In fact, go shout it. Scream it.

The context for this scripture text is astonishing, when you think about it, because it is written at a terrible time in the people's history. In 587BCE the kingdom of Judah has been overthrown by the Babylonians and the city of Jerusalem destroyed and abandoned. In response to this, the prophet writes this word of hope.

Beyond that, the context for reading it in Advent, and in the *via positiva* is no less astonishing. Traditionally, we read the passage in Advent and think of the coming of Christ, here seemingly foretold in the words that will be echoed by John the Baptist some 600 years later. But in the context of the *via positiva* there is another strength as well, because we are reminded of God's blessing, of God's desire to forgive us, to love us, to care for us, despite all that goes on.

The grass withers, the flowers fade. We are fickle. We disappoint.

Things do not always go according to plan—our plan or God's plan.

Yet the tendency of God is not to abandon, but to be present. In the midst of turmoil, God tells the heavenly assembly, "get out there and proclaim it: to every mountain and valley and all the people—to every living thing. I want all flesh to see and know that God is here, that God has not forgotten them."

God is coming. Not in power to destroy, but in awesome power to comfort.

Comfort.

It's from the Latin—*com* meaning "with" and *fort* meaning "strength."

To comfort is to strengthen, to shore up.

God is here to encourage. God comes with power and might we are told in verse 10.

And how is that power and might made manifest?

Lest we get excited or fearful and conjure up images of armies—so often the world's first reaction to words like power and might—the prophet makes it abundantly clear that God's way of showing power is to nurture. God comes as a shepherd to feed us and care for us, even gathering up the lambs most in need of care, and gently leading the mother sheep.

Not exactly a mean, punishing image, is it?

We may be fickle, swayed by the wind, but the word of God endures.

The word we met in Genesis.

The word that said "let there be" and things came into being.

The word that said "it is good" and it was so.

The word that still says "it is good."

December 2

John 1:1-5, 14, NRSV

> [1]In the beginning was the Word, and the Word was with God, and the Word was God. [2]He was in the beginning with God. [3]All things came into being through him, and without him not one thing came into being. What has come into being [4]in him was life, and the life was the light of all people.
>
> [5]The light shines in the darkness, and the darkness did not overcome it.
>
> [14]And the Word became flesh and lived among us, and we have seen his glory, the glory as of a father's only son, full of grace and truth.

I became aware that the song of universal grace was coming from the room, right where I was standing. It's a song felt more than heard, coming from even deeper than the heart.
—Sam Keen.

For my 13th birthday I received a copy of the New Testament. It had a bright and exciting cover, clearly intended to appeal to a budding teenager.

On the back, in fairly large letters, were the opening verses of the gospel of John. Only at the time, I didn't know that that's what they were. I just thought it was some pretty far out stuff that I'd never seen or heard before.

In the beginning was the Word.
And the Word was with God.
And the Word was God.

This was amazing, totally amazing.

What did these strange words mean?

As I have come to realize later in life, this is St. John's version of the Christmas story.

Okay, I'll grant you, it's not often portrayed on Christmas cards. And, while it would make for a great light and laser show, it would be a little difficult to render as a Christmas pageant involving angelic children in old bathrobes, cardboard wings, and tinsel halos. There's not a sheep to be found, let alone a mythical donkey, implicit innkeeper, or imagined camel.

Yet there is no question at all that this is a nativity story and, frankly, a rather fun one and, more definitely, a very real and earthy one.

This is the birth story of the Cosmic Christ. This is the story of Wisdom come to earth in human form.

Unlike Matthew and Luke, who seek to tell us certain aspects of the historical origins of Jesus of Nazareth, John wants us to grasp the powerful meaning behind the fact that the Wisdom of God—the Artisan, the Playful Child, the Word that proclaimed worlds into being—has come to "pitch his tent" in the midst of that same world.

That's the literal meaning for the Greek verb usually translated as "dwelt among" us—to pitch one's tent.

It's a great image that somehow brings the cosmic and the earthly together in a most delightful way. The rather heavenly and divine nature of the Word—so ethereal, so hard to grasp, so mystical—is right here, smack dab in the very midst of everything: in the midst of us, in the midst of the creation that it helped call into being so long before.

Lest there be any mistaking the creation as anything less than a worthy place to be, here God's Word is pleased to make a home.

Amongst us. In the midst of us: of you, and me.

The whole darned bunch of us.

For in this Word comes life, life for *all* people.

Not just a few. Not just the nice ones, or the pretty ones, or the worthy ones (whoever those might be).

All people.

In the beginning was the Word—a word that said "it is good."

And in case we forgot, that Word pitched a tent in our midst just to remind us.

December 3

John 1:1-5, 14, NRSV

> [1]In the beginning was the Word, and the Word was with God, and the Word was God. [2]He was in the beginning with God. [3]All things came into being through him, and without him not one thing came into being. What has come into being [4]in him was life, and the life was the light of all people.
>
> [5]The light shines in the darkness, and the darkness did not overcome it.
>
> [14]And the Word became flesh and lived among us, and we have seen his glory, the glory as of a father's only son, full of grace and truth.

The typical Christian uses language like "Jesus came into this world" as though he was a guest from another planet visiting on a temporary work visa.
—Bruce Sanguin

Someone in a confirmation class once asked the brilliant question, "Where did God get the idea for everything from?"

It had never dawned on me to ask that or even, so far as I could recall, wonder that.

But it's a great question.

Maybe the answer lies in John's gospel. Maybe one way to read it is: *In the beginning, God had an idea. And the idea was God's. In fact, it was a part of God. And one day, God decided to share that idea with the rest of the world.*

After all, what is an idea?

What is a thought?

What is a word—with or without a capital letter?

As this first week of Advent draws to a close, we also complete the first path, the *via positiva*. We have focused on, danced with, celebrated God's wonder-filled idea to create a world long ago, and not to abandon it, but to remain intimately involved with it.

Now we read that God's Word became flesh and dwelt among us, full of grace and truth.

Grace: something of such extreme and pure value you can never earn it, but it's freely given by God to all.

Truth: something greater than the sum of all the facts and data of the universe, yet dependent on none of them.

And this Word that lives among us is full of these things, and greater besides.

Whoa. It takes a minute to digest all of that.

So let's back up a few verses. We read that this light shines in the darkness, and that the darkness has not overcome it. That's important.

Because I don't know about you, but I find so many times lately that I run into people who are convinced that the "forces of evil" in this world are about to take over at any moment. Granted, there are some horrifying and appalling things out there and we can readily list them without much effort at all.

But to fear them to the point of paralysis, or to assume that they are even remotely capable of taking over is to underestimate the power of that stubborn glimmer of divine light that came not just once into the world, but that comes into the world with every act of faith, with every act of justice-laden defiance, with every breath of life given and every word spoken in God's name.

Because the light shines (not shone, but *shines)* in the darkness.

And the darkness has not overcome it.

If it hasn't yet, why would we dare assume it ever would? What does that say about how we understand God?

So here we are.

We have this Word, God's Word, coming into our world.

Coming not just for a visit, but to stay, to be fully present.

It's not just any word; it's a word full of grace and truth. A word so powerful it brought all creation into being and declared it to be good, and no manner of human evil or ingenuity has yet extinguished that Word.

Thus, emboldened by this wondrous truth, the power of God's word of blessing that has sustained us on the *via positiva*, we move into the next path.

Week Two:
the via negativa

*Have learned in the night
darkness is only a path,
a way around fear.*

December 4

Philippians 2:5-8, *THE MESSAGE*

> [5]Think of yourselves the way Christ Jesus thought of himself. [6]He had equal status with God but didn't think so much of himself that he had to cling to the advantages of that status no matter what. Not at all. [7]When the time came, he set aside the privileges of deity and took on the status of a slave, became human! Having become human, he stayed human. [8]It was an incredibly humbling process. He didn't claim special privileges. Instead, he lived a self-less, obedient life and then died a selfless, obedient death—and the worst kind of death at that: a crucifixion.

God is not found in the soul by adding anything, but by a process
of subtraction.
—Meister Eckhart

In this second week of Advent, we embark on the *via negativa*.

For most people the word "negative" has, well, negative connotations. But in the *via negativa* it helps to think of some other aspects of the word instead.

In the days prior to digital photography, cameras that used film produced a negative from which a print was made. The negative, rather than being anything wrong or bad, was simply the exact opposite of the final image. Where the photograph was to be black, the negative was white, and vice versa. The *via negativa* is sort of like that. It is the flip side of the *via positiva* and, as such, is a necessary part of the journey; it need not be feared.

The darkness is a mysterious place, where great things happen. Sleep and renewal and dreams occur in the dark of night. Seeds sprout and begin to grow in the dark of the earth. The promise of life begins to happen in the dark of the womb. So we embrace the dark and, in order to do that, we let go.

In the Christmas hymn *Joy to the World* we sing, "Let every heart prepare Christ room." Part of that preparation is to clear a space. We empty ourselves, we let go, so that we might allow God to enter.

The example we have, Paul tells the Philippians (and us) is none other than Jesus himself.

Philippians 2:5-11 has come to be known as one of the great hymns of the early church. But I'm not so sure Paul is writing about Christ here as much as Paul is writing about us. The key is in verse 5 which, in *Today's New International Version* reads, "in your relationships with one another, have the same attitude of mind Christ Jesus had." Paul goes on to say, in essence, "look, friends, if Jesus could let go of everything and become truly human (and he was God) then surely, you can let go of your egos and become truly human, can't you?"

Easier said than done.

It can be so hard to be human, to be humble.

They both come from the same root—the Latin word for earth. To be human, to be humble, is to be grounded. Not to be dirt or to let ourselves be treated like dirt (that is humiliation—there's a difference) but to *choose* to let go, to humble *ourselves* and become grounded, truly human.

Someone once said that it's hard to have your head in the clouds or your nose in the air if you've got both feet planted firmly on the ground. I think that's kind of what Paul is getting at here.

To quote Meister Eckhart, "where clinging to things ends is where God begins to be."[2]

When we can let go of our agendas, we can make room for God's. Jesus did it. Jesus modeled it for us.

Jesus models it for us by letting go of whatever it meant to be "in the very nature of God" (and if we get hung up trying to analyze Paul's Christology here I think we miss the point of the passage). Jesus models it for us by being born in a manger, to unwed parents of the peasant class, in a backwater town, in an occupied land. That's pretty humble.

Jesus models it for us by wandering around with social "outcasts" and "misfits" such as women and children and foreigners and the poor and the disabled and tax collectors and those labeled sinners and, in other words, anyone who has ever been disliked or discarded—or felt that way—by the world.

Can we empty ourselves?

Can we humble ourselves?

Can we become fully human?

Because that's what Jesus Christ did.

Jesus became fully human.

All the way—even to the point of death (and beyond).

That's all a part of Christmas.

It's all a part of Advent.

Welcome to the *via negativa*.

December 5

Matthew 3: 1-6, NRSV

¹In those days John the Baptist appeared in the wilderness of Judea, proclaiming, ²"Repent, for the kingdom of heaven has come near." ³This is the one of whom the prophet Isaiah spoke when he said, "The voice of one crying out in the wilderness: 'Prepare the way of the Lord, make his paths straight.'" ⁴Now John wore clothing of camel's hair with a leather belt around his waist, and his food was locusts and wild honey. ⁵Then the people of Jerusalem and all Judea were going out to him, and all the region along the Jordan, ⁶and they were baptized by him in the river Jordan, confessing their sins.

> *When true simplicity is gained,*
> *to bow and to bend we shan't be ashamed;*
> *to turn, turn will be our delight*
> *'til by turning, turning, we come round right.*
> *—Shaker hymn "Simple Gifts"*

I don't know about you, but I cringe a little bit when I hear the word "repent." However, I have tried very hard over the years to recapture a truer sense of this concept that can be so very helpful—indeed, vital—for the spiritual journey.

Like many of our faith words, "repent" and "repentance" have gotten a lot of bad press and misuse over the years, and it's really a shame. Because the thing that John the Baptist invites us to do is life-giving, transforming—not at all something to fear.

The Greek word that has been translated "repentance" has to do with changing one's mind—not just coming up with a new idea or deciding to do something different, but changing one's understanding and one's perceptions. In that sense, "repent" could be read as "change the way you're looking at things. Re-think how you view your world. Re-examine your life. Re-examine your priorities. And then change."

For me, that's a far cry from the image of a stern and angry preacher pointing a finger at me and implying that I am evil and bad, and must assume that everything I do is evil and bad, and I have to stop and confess or else.

I *do* need to re-examine. And I do need to change.

But wait: there's more.

You see, John the Baptist didn't speak Greek, the language that the New Testament was written in—he spoke Aramaic. And the Aramaic word for "repent" (which is sort of pronounced *tav)* is quite amazing. It has to do with turning or, more specifically, returning.

It's kind of like what the ocean waves do when they come in to shore, and then return to the greater ocean.

We move away from God. And prophets—like John—call us to return to God.

If we understand repentance this way, then we can readily understand the crowds that thronged to John beside the Jordan, eager for baptism and renewal. I don't think for one second that they went there out of fear. I myself would have gone there in hope, and in the assurance of a wonderful promise. According to this strange prophet, God was inviting me to stop what I was doing, and to return to the true source of my being.

This is the gift of the *via negativa:* that repentance is not something to be feared, but a genuine gift from God. For in the context of God's promises of forgiveness and new life, we can dare to look at, examine, and fully encounter all of life. The reality of it. The yin and the yang, or the "yippee" and the "yuck" as a friend of mine used to put it.

Because we have this invitation to be in constant examination, and the further invitation to turn and return to God. The ebb and flow of the divine ocean—as we move away from God, so God invites us, and pulls us, back.

Now it would be great if I didn't *have* to do this—that's what St. Paul struggles with so many times and writes about in several places. But that's what life is, and it helps to own it. Life has all manner of ups and downs and valleys and hills and proverbial rivers to cross and dragons to encounter and flowers to smell, and all that other stuff in between.

I need to look at all of my everything, and let go of what I do not need, what is holding me back from oneness with God, what is harming myself and others and the world around me, and the things I no longer need.

When I do this, I am forgiven, and I can move on. As Matthew Fox puts it, "Forgiveness is another word for letting go. We are saved by forgiveness, the power to forgive ourselves, to allow ourselves to be forgiven, which matures into the power to forgive others and allow them their time to be forgiven. Forgiveness is about letting go of guilt—some imagined, some real—and about letting go of fear. There is no healing, no salvation, without forgiveness. And with forgiveness all things become saved and healed once again. Creation is restored."[3]

Re-examine your priorities.

Return to God, the source of your life.

Repent.

December 6

Matthew 3: 7-1 2, THE MESSAGE

[7]When John realized that a lot of Pharisees and Sadducees were showing up for a baptismal experience because it was becoming the popular thing to do, he exploded: "Brood of snakes! What do you think you're doing slithering down here to the river? Do you think a little water on your snakeskins is going to make any difference? [8]It's your life that must change, not your skin! [9]And don't think you can pull rank by claiming Abraham as father. Being a descendant of Abraham is neither here nor there. Descendants of Abraham are a dime a dozen. [10]What counts is your life. Is it green and blossoming? Because if it's deadwood, it goes on the fire.

[11]"I'm baptizing you here in the river, turning your old life in for a kingdom life. The real action comes next: The main character in this drama—compared to him I'm a mere stagehand—will ignite the kingdom life within you, a fire within you, the Holy Spirit within you, changing you from the inside out. [12]He's going to clean house—make a clean sweep of your lives. He'll place everything true in its proper place before God; everything false he'll put out with the trash to be burned."

It's really easy to fall into the trap of believing that what we do *is more important than what we* are. *Of course, it's the opposite that's true: what we* are *ultimately determines what we* do!
—*Fred Rogers*

There's that repentance thing again, that wonderful gift whereby we can let go of the things that are weighing us down and slowing us down, things like ego and personal agendas and worries and anxieties.

The junk, the garbage. Most translations call it "chaff" or "husks."

Sin, if you like.

It's the stuff that keeps us from having a full relationship with God, the stuff that gets in the way, the stuff that distances us. What we call it doesn't matter. But we know what it is.

So what do we do with it? Let it go.

Right. Except it's not always that easy, is it?

I know I've grown quite fond of some of my bad habits, some of my favorite anxieties and petty agenda items. In good times I would be quite happy to let them go. However, at other times, I want to hold on for dear life. But what purpose do they serve me? None, if I stop to think about it.

They get in the way. They keep me from being the person God wants me to be.

Things like pride, self-centeredness, self-righteousness.

A sense of entitlement, a sense of holier-than-thou.

I don't like to admit those things, but they're there, no matter how hard I might try to deny, rationalize, rename, or redecorate.

And then John the Baptist challenges me, tells me to bear fruit that shows I've let go, that shows I've changed. How do I do that?

I have to trust God. I have to trust this Messiah that John talks about, who is coming to help me through this dilemma.

"His winnowing fork is in his hand."

Okay, what's that about?

Have you ever tried to rake leaves or grass on a windy day? The heavier ones go where you want them to go, but the lighter bits fly every which way. That's the chaff.

Jesus comes along to my life with a great big pitchfork, a rake, a winnowing fan or fork, and says, "Okay, let's sift through things and see what we have."

I, of course, have to be willing. It's a risky business. Those things—character defects we might call them—of which I've grown so very fond are on the block here. In the final analysis, they are of no inherent value. They do me no good, much as I might like them. Jealousy, greed, pride, self-serving nonsense—all the things that belong in the "sin" column—are really quite weightless, quite worthless.

If I will let go of them, and allow Jesus to do a wonderful shakedown of my life, those worthless non-values will fly away and land in a pile over there somewhere, out of reach. I'll be left with values that are of, well, value, of substance, things that will enable me to bear fruit worthy of repentance, to use John's phrase. Values that will allow me to live as God wants, gifts that will equip me to do the second-chance living that God has offered.

The chaff? The garbage?

Jesus will gather it up and burn it, fuel for a fire. Chaff in biblical times was used for cooking fuel, or for brick-making.

So, you see, even my worthless junk can find a use in the hands of Jesus Christ. If I will let go and let God (to use the Al-Anon slogan) amazing things can happen. Even my "sin" can bear fruit, can be somehow miraculously turned around and given purpose.

Matthew Fox borrowed an image from Japanese poet Kenji Miyazawa concerning the letting go of pain, and I think it applies here as well.

Firstly, we take our pain—or, in this case, our "sin," or those things which burden us, trouble us, and stand in the way of our relationship with God—and embrace it like a bundle of kindling for a fire. We hold it, we carry it for a time, and then we thrust it on a fire, letting it go. Christ will assist us in this, John assures us, and in the process we receive benefit from the warmth and light the fire can provide.[4]

Each of us knows, in our heart of hearts, the junk that keeps us from full relationship with God. When we are open and honest with God, Jesus Christ can help us rid ourselves of this junk. It is the chaff that Christ takes from us, and burns for our use and benefit.

And we move on.

December 7

Matthew 24: 3-1 4, NRSV

³When he was sitting on the Mount of Olives, the disciples came to him privately, saying, "Tell us, when will this be, and what will be the sign of your coming and of the end of the age?"

⁴Jesus answered them, "Beware that no one leads you astray. ⁵For many will come in my name, saying, 'I am the Messiah!' and they will lead many astray. ⁶And you will hear of wars and rumors of wars; see that you are not alarmed; for this must take place, but the end is not yet. ⁷For nation will rise against nation, and kingdom against kingdom, and there will be famines and earthquakes in various places: ⁸all this is but the beginning of the birthpangs.

⁹"Then they will hand you over to be tortured and will put you to death, and you will be hated by all nations because of my name. ¹⁰Then many will fall away, and they will betray one another and hate one another. ¹¹And many false prophets will arise and lead many astray. ¹²And because of the increase of lawlessness, the love of many will grow cold. ¹³But the one who endures to the end will be saved. ¹⁴And this good news of the kingdom will be proclaimed throughout the world, as a testimony to all the nations; and then the end will come.

Due to the lack of experienced trumpeters, the end of the world has been postponed for three weeks.
—Anonymous

I have encountered people—perhaps you have, too—who get excited at the prospect of the end of the world. I know some personally but, beyond that, I know there are millions of others because of the popularity of books such as the *Left Behind* series and other pop fiction stuff that tries to stir up fear, mistrust, and who knows what else.

The end of the world is big business. It sells, just like any other good, titillating scandal. People look for—and consequently, find—all manner of signs. But think about it: people have been finding these signs for thousands of years. However, to the best of my knowledge, the world has not yet come to an end. If it has, no one's told me.

Much of the fascination with the end of the world has to do with letting us off the hook. If things are coming to an end, then I need not take any responsibility for anything. I can mistreat the earth, other people, myself. I can make things right with God and then cross my fingers that it all ends quickly, before I botch things up again.

Except, somehow, I don't think that's the point. I don't think that's what living is about.

"Before the world ends," Jesus tells the disciples, "the gospel will be proclaimed."

That could take a while.

"Lots of false prophets will arise, too."

That would probably include those who try to claim that the world is ending.

"Love will be in short supply," according to one translation of Matthew 24:12.[5]

Nations will wage war, and earthquakes will happen, and sunrises and sunsets will occur, and rainstorms, and inflation, and pop stars will come and go. And through it all, the world will not end. Not for a while, anyway. *So hang in there,* Jesus says.

But we get scared. Life is, after all, pretty scary at times.

A certain amount of fear is healthy. Learning as a child to be afraid of a hot stove keeps us from burning ourselves. However, too much fear can paralyze us. It shuts us down.

Guilt can shut us down, too. And guilt is related to fear. Fear of what God might do to us for being "bad."

Guilt not only shuts us down, it keeps us from repentance. Guilt can keep us from turning around, from taking advantage of the second chance that God offers, from letting go of the chaff and garbage that keep us from a full relationship with God.

So we find ourselves needing to let go again. Let go of fear, let go of the desire to control, let go of needing to know the outcome.

What matters is not predicting the date of the end of the world, or even pondering its possibility. What matters is living in the now.

In a café in Sydney, Australia, I saw a clock that had no numbers, just hands. Across the clock face were the words "The time is now."

Live now. Proclaim the gospel with your living. Let go of the things that do not matter.

The placement of the celebration of Christmas at this time of year is not accidental.

The Bible gives absolutely no indication of when Jesus was born, and the early church did not celebrate his birth. It was the arrival of Christianity in northern Europe that brought about the addition of Christmas to the liturgical calendar, and it coincided with the winter solstice, at a time of year when the days in northern Europe were getting very short, and the hours of darkness increasingly long.

In the midst of this, Christian missionaries dared to suggest that people focus not on the increasing hours of cold and dark, but rather on the promise and presence of Christ as light of the world.

The *via negativa* is about living through those long, cold, fearful nights of unknowing. Not merely tolerating them, but trusting that in them, God is with us. We need to trust that the dark is in fact not a bad time, but a growing time, a dreaming time, a resting time.

There will be day and there will be night, Jesus says. There will be winter and summer, spring and fall. Ups and downs. Ins and outs. It doesn't matter, because God will be with you in all of it.

Embrace the dark, let go the fear, and in so doing, grow a little stronger, and a little warmer.

December 8

Hosea 11:1-11, THE MESSAGE

[1]"When Israel was only a child, I loved him.
  I called out, 'My son!'—called him out of Egypt.
[2]But when others called him,
  he ran off and left me.
He worshiped the popular sex gods,
  he played at religion with toy gods.
[3]Still, I stuck with him. I led Ephraim.
  I rescued him from human bondage,
[4]But he never acknowledged my help,
  never admitted that I was the one pulling his wagon,
That I lifted him, like a baby, to my cheek,
  that I bent down to feed him.
[5]Now he wants to go back to Egypt or go over to Assyria—
  anything but return to me!
[6]That's why his cities are unsafe—the murder rate sky-rockets
  and every plan to improve things falls to pieces.
[7]My people are hell-bent on leaving me.
  They pray to god Baal for help.
  He doesn't lift a finger to help them.
[8]But how can I give up on you, Ephraim?
  How can I turn you loose, Israel?
How can I leave you to be ruined like Admah,
  devastated like luckless Zeboim?
I can't bear to even think such thoughts.
My insides churn in protest.
[9]And so I'm not going to act on my anger.
  I'm not going to destroy Ephraim.

And why? Because I am God and not a human.

I'm The Holy One and I'm here—in your very midst.
[10]"The people will end up following GOD.

I will roar like a lion—

Oh, how I'll roar!
[11]My frightened children will come running from the west.

Like frightened birds they'll come from Egypt,
from Assyria like scared doves.

I'll move them back into their homes."
GOD's Word!

> *I like you because of…*
> *I love you in spite of…*
> —*Anonymous*

"Why do you care?" the young man asked me.

At first, I thought it was a silly question. Until I tried to answer it.

"Because" seemed kind of empty, kind of trite. But it was the best I could offer.

And so I answered, "Because it's what I do."

"Why?" he persisted.

"Because it's what I know."

"But it doesn't make sense."

"It doesn't have to make sense. It's because I love you."

"But why do you love me?"

"Because."

The conversation went on, and it was, in many ways, one of the most difficult conversations of my life. Not because it was inherently painful, or anything of the sort, but because I realized that there *are* no real answers. There are no explanations for loving, for caring.

Various allegories are drawn in scripture for the relationship between God and the people. The prophet Hosea uses the image of God as parent, and the nation as a child—a rebellious teenager by the sounds of things. Perhaps you are a parent who has said similar things to a child, or heard something like this spoken to you:

> *When you were a child, I loved you, and I called you out of danger. But the more I called, the more you ran away. You disregarded my values, everything I stood for. I cared for you; I fed you, and clothed you, and stayed up with you at night when you were sick or having bad dreams. And how do you repay me? You'd rather spend your time running off with those good-for-nothings who will lead you to ruin.*
>
> *So, fine, if that's the way you want to be—get out of here! You want to live somewhere else? Do it! Take your stuff and go. Try to make it on your own, and see how you do.*

There are those times when we want to slam the door on someone. More to the point, there may be those times when we have felt as though God were slamming the door on us. If we were to stop reading Hosea 11 at verse 6, we might get that impression. But that's not where the passage ends. God has more to say to this rebellious child:

> *You seem bent on ignoring me. I phone, and you never answer. You won't reply my e-mails.*

> *And yet I cannot give up on you. How could I do that? It would sicken me to the very depths of my being. I will not act on my anger. I cannot do it. No matter what you might do to me, I will always love you.*
> *Always.*

Part of the faith journey, part of the *via negativa*, is to confront the reality of our moving away from God, and our returning to God. If we understand sin to be the state we find ourselves in when we move away from God, then it is important to recognize that we frequently travel into that place.

Sin is not the state of being "bad" or "evil" but rather the state of being detached, separated, from God. Running away, drifting away. We might do it consciously or unconsciously. But we do it.

The important piece is to own it, and not feel guilty about it. Guilt, as we observed in looking at Matthew 24, tends to move us further away from God, by making us continue feeling like we are "bad."

We are not bad. But we are capable, each and every one of us, of doing "bad" things. Wrong things. Hurtful things.

Owning them, apologizing, trying to make them right, trying to find ways to change and not do them again—all of these are ways of reconnecting with God.

It helps, as well, to remember that God is not sitting at home waiting for us in anger, ready to slap us and send us to our room, but rather—like the parent in the story of the prodigal son—comes running to welcome us.

"I can't stay angry with you," God says.

We are accountable for our actions, without question. Yet God still loves us.

Always.

Just because.

December 9

Hosea 11: 1-4, THE MESSAGE

> [1]"When Israel was only a child, I loved him.
>   I called out, 'My son!'—called him out of Egypt.
> [2]But when others called him,
>   he ran off and left me.
> He worshiped the popular sex gods,
>   he played at religion with toy gods.
> [3]Still, I stuck with him. I led Ephraim.
>   I rescued him from human bondage,
> [4]But he never acknowledged my help,
>   never admitted that I was the one pulling his wagon,
> That I lifted him, like a baby, to my cheek,
>   that I bent down to feed him.

I believe that at the center of the universe there dwells a loving spirit who longs for all that's best in all of creation, a spirit who knows the great potential of each planet as well as each person, and little by little will love us into being more than we ever dreamed possible. That loving spirit would rather die than give up on any one of us.
—Fred Rogers

One of the most difficult things in parenting is letting go. The classic image of a mother bird pushing babies out of the nest, knowing that some of them will fall as they learn to fly, strikes a chord.

Who wants to do that?

Yet we must.

Perhaps that's what the "fall" story was really about, back in the Garden of Eden. Not so much about the presence of evil in the world as about the tension of running from God, and feeling pushed out, and wanting independence, and wanting to stay home, and needing to go away, and, and … it's that whole teenager thing again.

Letting go of a child is hard. Watching them fall as they learn to walk is not an easy task, yet it is a necessary part of the process. Failure is part of learning, as much as night is part of day, and doubt a part of faith. In fact, it isn't really failure at all—it's simply another attempt. Some attempts get us where we want to be, and some don't.

God takes a great risk in allowing us to be, and thus in allowing us to fail, and thus in allowing us to turn away.

It all begins with teaching us to walk, really. That's what started the whole independence bit. Without that, we could never have gotten very far. Yet, we also would not be human. I'm not sure what we would be, but we would not be the creatures that God intended.

Let me be clear: I'm not meaning *walk* literally, any more than Hosea is. It does not matter how we are mobile—the key thing is that God, patiently and lovingly and gently, taught us how to be independent. God gave us the ability to think for ourselves, and do for ourselves, and—in a word—*be* ourselves.

At the same time, God challenged us to love one another and care for one another, to tend the garden (read: planet earth, and the rest of the universe) and, hopefully, remember the one who created us and loved us, who bent down to feed us.

But more than anything, God gave us the freedom to make mistakes.

That's it in a nutshell. God gave us the ability to wander off in search of who-knows-what, and to fall down and skin our knees in the process.

Do you ever think how painful that must be for God?

God has to watch us make mistakes, day in and day out, without intervening and enabling. What an absolute nightmare.

I rather imagine God as divine parent sitting up at nights, hoping we come home safe and sound. Those voices of conscience that we hear sometimes are like God leaving a note on the kitchen table, reminding us to be careful, or gently suggesting we might want to have a change of heart about some plan or another.

God watches us go in and out of the garden, and probably mutters under the divine breath, "please make the right choice this time."

And then God lets go.

That's the amazing thing of it.

If we are bent on doing our own thing, God allows it. God set things up that way, the story seems to be telling us.

For whatever reason, for better or worse, the world that spins aimlessly in space does so on its own axis. God set it in motion, surely, but we are not puppets. We are free to run away, to do our own thing.

The good news is, when *we* let go, and invite God into the equation, wondrous things can happen.

When we stop trying to turn the world our way, God's way can take shape again.

Made in the image of God, we are challenged to do the very thing that God has done: to let go.

December 10

Philippians 2: 5-1 1, NRSV

> [5]Let the same mind be in you that was in Christ Jesus,
> [6]who, though he was in the form of God,
>   did not regard equality with God
>   as something to be exploited,
> [7]but emptied himself,
>   taking the form of a slave,
>   being born in human likeness.
> And being found in human form,
> [8]he humbled himself
>   and became obedient to the point of death—
>   even death on a cross.
> [9]Therefore God also highly exalted him
>   and gave him the name that is above every name,
> [10]so that at the name of Jesus
>   every knee should bend,
>   in heaven and on earth and under the earth,
> [11]and every tongue should confess
>   that Jesus Christ is Lord, to the glory of God the
>   Father.

I would like to be simply a puddle of water reflecting the light of
the sky.
—Dom Helder Camara

Recently, His Holiness the Dalai Lama visited our community. While most people were excited and amazed that someone of this stature would come to visit, others got upset.

"Why was all this fuss being made?" they wanted to know. "No one made this fuss when so-and-so came to town" and then they referred to a well-known Christian evangelist.

It was a question that piqued the curiosity of someone like me, a Christian who affirms deep ecumenism (what some might call inter-faith dialogue).

The difference seemed obvious. The Dalai Lama, while a Buddhist, frequently encourages people not to convert to Buddhism, but to live out to the fullest the faith they already have. In sharing his beliefs, convictions, and understandings of life, he repeatedly celebrates his own faith story, while affirming and encouraging those of others.

Contrast this with many evangelists of other religions—not just Christian—who tend to speak from a stance of "I/we have a monopoly on the truth, and you need to accept my/our version of it because it is the only one that can save you."

Bit of a difference, don't you think?

Writing to his friends in Philippi, Paul encourages them to have the same mind that Christ had. In other words: be humble. Be Christ-like, which amounts to the same thing.

Now let's face it, Paul—like the Dalai Lama centuries later—is unabashedly proud of his faith.

All of creation—the plums and the snakes and the pomegranates and the elephants and the clouds and the waterfalls—will some day recognize the goodness that is in Jesus Christ. All creation will one day know that it is Jesus, the cosmic Christ, to whom they owe their life.

This is a bold and wonderful statement.

Yet it's not quite the same as saying "some day everyone will be a Christian and think like me."

Maybe an analogy helps. I like chocolate. In fact, I love chocolate and I am quite capable of raving madly over some exquisite chocolate desert as being the greatest thing in the world. I love it so much that I cannot, frankly, understand why someone else would not want to taste it, to savor it, to enjoy it.

However, there are people who don't care for chocolate at all. If I were to say "you *must* try this. It's the greatest thing there is," that does not make it factually true. But it certainly lets others know that I am passionate about it.

The same with this letter to the Philippians. Why wouldn't Paul want everything in creation to acknowledge the goodness of Christ?

Christ Jesus has completely transformed Paul's life, and that of many of his friends, and in the context of that time and place Christianity offered the only viable alternative to the tyranny of Rome. But that does *not* necessarily imply that Paul means a literal, exclusionary faith stance here. Paul simply wants—albeit with great passion—the whole world to find what he has found.

Beyond that, however, is something deeper.

The Christ that is being celebrated here is a humble Christ, one who is poured out.

Christ's "reward" for humility and selflessness is to be recognized as God. Kind of ironic—you put yourself up on a pedestal, and you will get knocked down. You humble yourself, and you will be lifted up.

Oh yeah, Jesus said that sometimes, didn't he?

Creation—God's creation—is a life cycle of self-giving. Through birth and rebirth, through erosion and decay which yield new life, the cosmos is always regenerating. It does so in a process of giving up, of pouring out.

This is what it means to be Christ-like. This is what it means to be a part of the cosmos.

To grasp after godliness—to eat that apple so we know everything, to shortcut the universe by building a tower up to the heavens, to ignore those around us in a mad dash for personal salvation—all of these things are not Christ-like.

The "mind" of Christ, shown to us in the birth, living, dying, and rising of Jesus, is one of giving: giving up, giving out, giving away.

Perhaps the hope in this passage is not so much that everyone will become Christian as that those of us who claim to follow Christ will recognize his selfless example, see it around us in all of creation, and emulate it.

Who knows what could happen then.

Week Three:
via creativa

Daring brokenness
shattered truths regroup themselves.
Behold: all things new.

December 11

Isaiah 2: 1-5, NRSV

[1]The word that Isaiah son of Amoz saw concerning Judah and Jerusalem.
[2]In days to come
    the mountain of the Lord's house
shall be established as the highest of the mountains,
    and shall be raised above the hills;
all the nations shall stream to it.
[3]Many peoples shall come and say,
"Come, let us go up to the mountain of the LORD,
    to the house of the God of Jacob;
that he may teach us his ways
    and that we may walk in his paths."
For out of Zion shall go forth instruction,
    and the word of the LORD from Jerusalem.
[4]He shall judge between the nations,
    and shall arbitrate for many peoples;
they shall beat their swords into plowshares,
    and their spears into pruning hooks;
nation shall not lift up sword against nation,
neither shall they learn war any more.
[5]O house of Jacob,
    come, let us walk
    in the light of the LORD!

> *There is a crack in everything,*
> *that's where the light gets in.*
> *—Leonard Cohen*

I lived in Quebec for several years, and was intrigued with the French expression *allons-y*. It's used for "let's go" but it literally means "let's go there." I love the fact that it contains a sense of direction, as if we know where we are going.

Not just a generic "let's go wherever," but a sense of purpose.

Let's go.

Let's go up the mountain of God.

Let's go into the *via creativa*.

Matthew Fox points out that all of the paths of Creation Spirituality find their apex in this third path, the *via creativa*, so it is fitting that we have a mountain to work with.[6] The *via positiva* and the *via negativa* both lead here, and the *via transformativa* flows away from here.

This isn't just any mountain, it's God's mountain—the mountain of God's temple.

For the ancients of many cultures, mountains were places not only of contemplation, but of meeting God. For the ancient Hebrews, the temple was *the* place for meeting God. It is a place of reconciliation, a place of breakthrough. That's what the *via creativa* is all about.

In this part of our spiritual journey, God breaks in. It is where we embrace the divine—both outside of ourselves and within.

We are returning to God. We know where we are going, because in the *via positiva* we recognized and reclaimed our divine goodness. In the *via negativa* we owned our pain, and let go of the things that keep us from God. Now, we go up to the mountain of God, and flow back to the source of our life (note the curious use of the word "streaming" in v. 2).

This is where we belong—in the presence of God. Not that there is anywhere that is *not* in God's presence, but here we are making a conscious, intentional effort to be in God's presence.

Who goes?

All nations.

Everyone, Isaiah says, will come streaming to God's temple. Again, as in the reading from Philippians, this is not about converting the whole world to our belief system, but rather about celebrating the openness of God's invitation, the wonder of God's community. No longer will we perceive ourselves as belonging to a little club, reserved only for those who think like us and look like us and act like us. One day, we will recognize that God has invited everybody.

This is a new creation, our recognition that all people are invited into the divine presence, into the place of reconciliation with the divine and with one another, that we might begin something new.

What will we do when we get there? We will learn God's ways.

We will learn again to be creators, from none other than the Creator of the universe. Many of us have lost not so much the ability to create, but the will to create, the desire, or the awareness of our worth and giftedness. Society, peer pressure, or the powers of the world have too often told us that we are not the artists that God created us to be. We may not be Picasso, Emily Dickenson, Beethoven, or Judy Chicago—but we are all artists, for we are made in the image of the creator of all. And "we are God's work of art" (Ephesians 2:10).

Hosea spoke of God teaching us to walk, and how we then wandered away. Now Isaiah speaks about us coming back to God. Having emptied ourselves, we turn to God to be renewed and filled with divine energy.

We learn God's ways, ways that lead to peace.

Come, let's go up the mountain of God.

Come, let's journey in the light of God.

December 12

Isaiah 2: 4-5, NRSV

> [4][God] shall judge between the nations,
>   and shall arbitrate for many peoples;
> they shall beat their swords into plowshares,
>   and their spears into pruning hooks;
> nation shall not lift up sword against nation,
> neither shall they learn war any more.
> [5]O house of Jacob,
>   come, let us walk
>   in the light of the LORD!

During "the troubles" in Northern Ireland, a mediator walked into a negotiating session between Protestant and Roman Catholic factions wearing a T-shirt that read, "Don't shoot, I'm Jewish." The atmosphere lightened up immediately, and talks moved beyond an impasse.
—News item

If you are of a generation who, like me, grew up watching Monty Python's Flying Circus, you probably remember occasional scenes of John Cleese sitting behind a TV announcer's desk, completely straight-faced, announcing in a bland voice "and now for something completely different."

It's kind of what Isaiah said thousands of years before, when he invited all peoples to go up God's mountain and learn of God's ways.

Something quite different.

Something quite wonderful.

Isaiah talks about beating swords and spears into gardening tools. It's a powerful image, one so great that a statue of someone hammering a sword into a plowshare stands outside of the United Nations building in New York City.

This is what happens, the prophet says, when all nations stream into the presence of God—we learn the ways of peace, rather than the ways of war. We learn to care for creation (including one another) rather than destroy creation (including one another).

It helps if we bring this passage a little closer to home. Because, let's face it, many of us don't have swords or spears. Not literal ones, anyway.

And yet ...

If I think of swords and spears as those thoughts I have about harming others, or about wishing them harm, I realize that I am part of the problem.

I am not in control of a nation, I am not about to go to war against anyone or launch a nuclear attack or drop a bomb. Yet this passage applies directly to me because I have thoughts—and actions—that need conversion.

The breakthrough, the *via creativa* in this text, is the realization that learning God's ways means taking those habits, those ways of thinking and living that are demeaning and destructive of both myself and other creatures, and turning them around.

Some examples might help.

As a teenager I was mesmerized by the story of *Romeo and Juliet*. Part of it was seeing Franco Zeffirelli's film on a school field trip, but even more was the idea that these two teenagers, in foolishness and innocence, challenged the world around them. While their families were fighting a death feud for reasons long forgotten, these two young people discovered that they were human beings, not enemies, and fell in love. At the end, the prince notes that "with their death, they buried their parents' strife."

In the 1999 British film "Get Real" high school student Steven Carter stands before a school assembly and talks about the struggle of growing up gay. Steven closes his remarks by asking, "it's only love; what's everyone so afraid of?"

Several years ago, the church school resource *Seasons of the Spirit* included a poster called "Urban Pioneer." It showed a young child in the inner city, proudly holding a rather scraggly plant in a bucket. The child was standing in a paved parking lot, surrounded by apartment buildings.

I used this poster in a workshop with a group of church leaders. In the midst of the discussion, one woman spoke up and said, "I think it's an image of God."

We looked at her for more information, and she continued:

"God comes into our lives, and challenges us to see hope where there doesn't appear to be any. God comes in and says, 'do something. Plant a tree, even in the city. Turn a parking lot into a garden.'"

The images of students in the 1960's placing flowers in the gun barrels of the United States national guard; the photograph of the defiant student standing in front of the tank in

Tiananmen square; other images and stories of "random acts of kindness" and defiance of powers that destroy life—all these things are the stuff of turning swords into plowshares and spears into pruning hooks.

In the beginning God invited (commanded? challenged? encouraged?) us to care for the garden, to be stewards of creation.

We didn't do it—how well we know that story.

Now, says Isaiah, let us learn God's ways, and re-make ourselves into gardeners again.

December 13

Genesis 9: 8-1 7, NRSV

8Then God said to Noah and to his sons with him, 9"As for me, I am establishing my covenant with you and your descendants after you, 10and with every living creature that is with you, the birds, the domestic animals, and every animal of the earth with you, as many as came out of the ark. 11I establish my covenant with you, that never again shall all flesh be cut off by the waters of a flood, and never again shall there be a flood to destroy the earth."

12God said, "This is the sign of the covenant that I make between me and you and every living creature that is with you, for all future generations: 13I have set my bow in the clouds, and it shall be a sign of the covenant between me and the earth. 14When I bring clouds over the earth and the bow is seen in the clouds, 15I will remember my covenant that is between me and you and every living creature of all flesh; and the waters shall never again become a flood to destroy all flesh. 16When the bow is in the clouds, I will see it and remember the everlasting covenant between God and every living creature of all flesh that is on the earth." 17God said to Noah, "This is the sign of the covenant that I have established between me and all flesh that is on the earth."

A rainbow is a rainbow only and precisely because it is made up of different colors. We are placed on earth to discover that we are made for togetherness, for interdependence, for complementarity.
—*Archbishop Desmond Tutu*

What a great word: "complementarity."

I don't care that my computer's spellchecker doesn't like it—I think it's brilliant.

The rainbow, with all of its vibrant colors, coming after a light drizzle or a torrential downpour, can remind us of the unity and diversity, the complementarity, of God's creation.

And it reminds God not to destroy it.

Sometimes we skip over that part of the story, but it is right there in the text. "Whenever *I* see the rainbow," God says, "*I* will remember the covenant, and not destroy the earth." The rainbow, initially, is to serve as a sticky note posted on God's memo-board. "Note to self: do not destroy creation with a flood."

The reasons behind the flood are not important at this point in the story; the issue is the promise, the covenant, and all that it entails. It gets summed up so neatly in that rainbow.

Why a bow?

In earth science years ago we learned about raindrops, and the refraction of light, and the necessity of the arc-shape that the rainbow takes. But I didn't do very well in science, and I've forgotten how all of that works.

Just as well, because there's a powerful symbolism that serves us well.

"I have set my bow in the clouds," God says.

One quick glance at its shape, and we know we're not talking here about the kind of bow with which one would tie up hair or a package, or even one's shoes. This is the shape of a bow with which one would shoot arrows.

God has hung up a weapon in the sky.

God has, in effect, turned a sword into a plowshare.

Long before Isaiah challenged us to do the same thing, God says, "I am putting my weapon away. This destruction business—it's not working. It's not my style."

Funny (in a sad, ironic, tragic, intriguing use of the word "funny"—not in the laughing sense) that there are so many religious people in the world, of all religions, who are so excitable at the prospect of a destructive God. Yet here, almost at the very beginning of Genesis, God—after experimenting with expelling us from the garden for being a bit over-reaching, and destroying the earth with a flood—hangs up the divine weaponry in the sky and says, "I'm putting it away. I'm converting it to a technicolor thing of purest beauty. When we—you and I—see the rainbow, we'll stop. Together. And we'll remember that I, your God, promised not to destroy you."

What remains to be seen is what we do with our side of the rainbow.

On the other side of it, regardless of what God sees us doing here, God is reminded of the promise part of the covenant. On our side, when we look at the rainbow … do we see God? We tend to notice creation—everything is a bit greener, fresher. If we were not particularly keen to have the rain, then we're at least glad it's over. If we welcomed it, then we are already in a cheerful mood. Either way, we tend to look at a rainbow and be moved to joy. It draws our heart into a cosmic dance with the divine, at least for a moment.

What next?

Business as usual?

Or can we take a moment to celebrate the creation we see, and be reminded of the covenant, too? Of our part to love God, and one another as we love ourselves?

Can we pause for a moment and hang up a weapon, put it out of reach, turn it into a thing of beauty? Can we take our bow—with which we were perhaps going to fire a shot in anger at someone—and turn it instead into a means for making someone's day a little brighter, a little more joyous, and in so doing, color the world a little?

In this amazing cosmic moment wherein sunlight and raindrops interact in just the right balance, like a prism, to create this thing of beauty, God says, "remember ..."

December 14

Genesis 9: 8-1 7, THE MESSAGE

⁸Then God spoke to Noah and his sons: ⁹"I'm setting up my covenant with you including your children who will come after you, ¹⁰along with everything alive around you—birds, farm animals, wild animals—that came out of the ship with you. ¹¹I'm setting up my covenant with you that never again will everything living be destroyed by floodwaters; no, never again will a flood destroy the Earth."

¹²God continued, "This is the sign of the covenant I am making between me and you and everything living around you and everyone living after you. ¹³I'm putting my rainbow in the clouds, a sign of the covenant between me and the Earth. ¹⁴From now on, when I form a cloud over the Earth and the rainbow appears in the cloud, ¹⁵I'll remember my covenant between me and you and everything living, that never again will floodwaters destroy all life. ¹⁶When the rainbow appears in the cloud, I'll see it and remember the eternal covenant between God and everything living, every last living creature on Earth."

¹⁷And God said, "This is the sign of the covenant that I've set up between me and everything living on the Earth.

God, I can push the grass apart and lay my finger on thy heart.
—Edna St. Vincent Millay

Several years ago, the United Church of Canada revised its statement of faith. Properly known as *The New Creed*, it appears in the hymnals and worship books of many denominations around the world, but often not in its most current form.

The revision to which I am referring occurred in 1994, and added the line "to live with respect in creation."

At the time, I struggled with the line.

The fact that I don't struggle with it any more speaks volumes to me about where I have journeyed over the years in my faith development, and my awareness of my relationship with God and the cosmos.

But at the time, I struggled.

At the time, I would have preferred something like, "to live with respect for creation" or "to live in harmony with creation."

You see, I could accept creation was a thing, and that I was a thing. But we were different things, quite distinct from each other, turning at a different pace, evolving at a different pace. It was almost as if creation and I were living separate lives.

When I studied for my Doctor of Ministry degree, I was concerned about taking a class on cosmology. First of all, I wasn't exactly sure what cosmology was. But, beyond that, it sounded like science, and I had never been very good at that. I barely passed high school physics—I think because the teacher knew that if he didn't pass me, he'd have to put up with me for another semester.

I had no problem with science, I just didn't get it. But if I wanted to earn my DMin, I had to take cosmology. So, I took a science class, and this time I got it.

I got it because the professor shared it as story.

I got it because the professor explained a scientific view of the world—the universe, the cosmos—of which I was a part. It mattered. *I* mattered. The world would turn differently if I were not here, and I wouldn't exist but for everything in the universe. We were, in a word, related. All of us. Everything. Me and the goats and the rocks and the trees and the meteorites and the plankton and the chickens.

It was all pretty cosmic.

Literally.

I didn't fully understand it in an academic, explain-it-with-formulas-on-the-chalkboard kind of way, but I got it.

Science made sense because I came to realize that the primal flaring forth (some call it the big bang) that happened 15 billion years ago, and which through the wonders of evolution has yielded you and me, was also the moment when God picked up mud and breathed into it.

One and the same.

Some friends were watching Carl Sagan's DVD series *The Cosmos*. One person was quite disturbed by some of the implications of this broad understanding of creation on his previously-limited worldview. "Does this mean I'm nothing more than space dust?" he explained.

"Yes," someone else responded, "but think of it—we all are!"

God establishes a covenant with every living creature on earth. With all of life. With all of creation. We are each of us a part of it—none greater, none lesser.

For many groups of people in the world, the rainbow has become a powerful symbol of unity, of strength, of solidarity. The way in which it symbolically includes all colors equally, makes it a fitting emblem for any peoples struggling for acceptance and recognition. Archbishop Desmond Tutu spoke of everyone as "the rainbow people of God."

The rainbow symbolizes unity, diversity, life, hope, promise, hope in the face of a destructive world.

That's what it means to live with respect in creation.

We are all a part of creation, each of us—each person, thing, animal, each being—made in the image of God.

We are called upon to respect one another, to care for one another. And in so doing, maintain the balance that was/is the divine intention for the cosmos.

December 15

Luke 4:1 6-2 1, THE MESSAGE

[16][Jesus] came to Nazareth where he had been reared. As he always did on the Sabbath, he went to the meeting place. When he stood up to read, [17]he was handed the scroll of the prophet Isaiah. Unrolling the scroll, he found the place where it was written,
[18]God's Spirit is on me;
    he's chosen me to preach the Message of good news to the poor,
Sent me to announce pardon to prisoners and
    recovery of sight to the blind,
To set the burdened and battered free,
[19]to announce, "This is God's year to act!"
[20]He rolled up the scroll, handed it back to the assistant, and sat down. Every eye in the place was on him, intent. [21]Then he started in, "You've just heard Scripture make history. It came true just now in this place."

If you have come here to help me, you are wasting your time …
but if you have come because your liberation is bound up with
mine, then let us work together."
—Aboriginal Activists Group, Queensland, 1970's

There is no us and them, my partner always says, only us.

That seems to be what Jesus is trying to say in this passage, quoting the prophet Isaiah several hundred years before.

God's Spirit is upon me to proclaim good news.

We are beginning to move through the *via creativa* and into the *via transformativa*. We stop seeing ourselves in relationship to other people as subject/object, but as equals.

Just as we do not see ourselves as separate from creation, we stop seeing ourselves as distinct from others in terms of us/them. It does not mean, of course, that we give up our individuality. But we give up our superiority, our sense of distance. When we do that, we also give up any sense of giving that stems from pity.

We take on compassion.

Interesting word, compassion. The source is ambiguous.

The *com* part is Latin for *with*. But *passion* stems from *passus,* which has roots in both suffering and walking.

We generally think of compassion in terms of suffering together, sharing one another's suffering. That's a good understanding.

Yet also helpful is the idea of walking together, sharing one another's journey. Think of *compass*—the thing that goes around, in terms of helping us draw a circle in which everyone can fit.

Think of *compass*—the thing that points us in the right direction.

Think of *encompass*—to include, to embrace.

Sharing the journey together, being together, being at one with another—in joy, and in suffering.

Another word of interest is the English word "caring" which comes from the ancient Gothic word *kara*, meaning "lament." Caring is not so much something that we do for someone else, but rather joining someone in their lamenting.[7]

In the synagogue in Nazareth Jesus expresses an experience of breakthrough. The Spirit intercepts—breaks through, barges in—and challenges us to do the work of proclamation: with our words, and with our lives.

This scripture calls us to solidarity, to presence.

That is proclamation.

To me, it's different than preaching. Preaching implies "at" or "to" an object. (That doesn't necessarily make it wrong, by the way, it's just the way I understand or define it.)

Proclaiming, on the other hand, has more to do with making a declaration with one's whole being—investing one's self into the statement being made. It's not just words, but beliefs and action all rolled into one.

Proclaim good news to the poor, by living it.

All of us.

Together.

December 16

Luke 4:1 6-2 1, NRSV

> [16]When [Jesus] came to Nazareth, where he had been brought up, he went to the synagogue on the Sabbath day, as was his custom. He stood up to read, [17]and the scroll of the prophet Isaiah was given to him. He unrolled the scroll and found the place where it was written:
> [18]"The Spirit of the Lord is upon me,
>> because he has anointed me to bring good news to the poor.
>
> He has sent me to proclaim release to the captives
>> and recovery of sight to the blind,
>
> to let the oppressed go free,
> [19]to proclaim the year of the Lord's favor."
> [20]And he rolled up the scroll, gave it back to the attendant, and sat down. The eyes of all in the synagogue were fixed on him. [21]Then he began to say to them, "Today this scripture has been fulfilled in your hearing."

Any love or compassion which entails looking down on the other is not genuine compassion. To be genuine, compassion must be based on respect for the other, and on the realization that others have the right to be happy and overcome suffering just as much as you. On this basis, since you can see that others are suffering, you develop a genuine sense of concern for them.
—His Holiness the Dalai Lama

Jesus says that God's spirit has come upon him, and then states: "today this scripture is fulfilled in your hearing."

Each time we read this passage, each time we encounter it, each time we embody it, take it in and make it a part of us, it comes alive: the good news is proclaimed.

I once participated in an event where we read this scripture aloud several times, each time inserting the name of a different person who was present. I heard a group of people say, "The Spirit of God is upon Donald, because God has anointed Donald to proclaim good news to the poor," and on it went.

The experience was profound. Firstly, it was a joyous blessing to hear the affirmation that God's Spirit was upon me.

Secondly, it was an awesome responsibility to hear the commission divinely given to me, to proclaim nothing less than the reign of God in my world, in our world, in God's world.

This is what Jesus means when he says that the reign of God is at hand, that it has arrived, that it is within and among us. As we encounter and embody the message, the Word, the Spirit, the Sophia, the Wisdom of God, and make it a part of our being and our living—in other words, when we allow it to break through—then the reign of God happens. The empire of God spreads, challenging, permeating, and defeating the imperial powers of the world.

I wonder if Jesus' statement that "this has been fulfilled" is a little like his mother's prophetic declaration earlier in Luke's gospel, about all of the things God "has done."

In theory, everyone hearing Jesus that day could have ignored him, could have ignored the text that he read. Yet we are told, as the passage continues, that they were transfixed by Jesus' statement, impressed with his reading. It was only as he continued to expound on the text that their reaction turned to anger, so extreme in fact that they wanted to kill him.

Why?

Undoubtedly because he struck a chord.

And that's probably why Jesus said what he did, because he knew that they couldn't do nothing. (Yes, I intended the double negative there.)

In other words, they would have to do something.

At least someone would be moved to take seriously what Jesus said, to be moved to compassion, to embody truly the spirit that was proclaimed, and to act upon it.

And at that point, Jesus' statement becomes a fact: the scripture *has been* fulfilled. Because the process has begun. There is no turning back.

"Both the individual and the community come alive by this rekindling of the divine spark or seed or image in each of us," Matthew Fox said. "This is no small blessing for the individual or for society or for the ongoing cosmos itself. If we fail to love it well, it will return with cosmic fury to teach us, if nothing else, a respect that will never be forgotten."[8]

The Spirit of God is upon us: to proclaim the gospel, and in so doing to bring about the reign of God in our world.

Nothing more.

Nothing less.

December 17

Romans 8:14-22, NRSV

[14]For all who are led by the Spirit of God are children of God. [15]For you did not receive a spirit of slavery to fall back into fear, but you have received a spirit of adoption. When we cry, "Abba! Father!" [16]it is that very Spirit bearing witness with our spirit that we are children of God,

[17]and if children, then heirs, heirs of God and joint heirs with Christ—if, in fact, we suffer with him so that we may also be glorified with him. [18]I consider that the sufferings of this present time are not worth comparing with the glory about to be revealed to us. [19]For the creation waits with eager longing for the revealing of the children of God; [20]for the creation was subjected to futility, not of its own will but by the will of the one who subjected it, in hope [21]that the creation itself will be set free from its bondage to decay and will obtain the freedom of the glory of the children of God. [22]We know that the whole creation has been groaning in labor pains until now …

And when did God—as opposed to society and its leaders—ever
excuse any of us from being an active, energetic image of God?
—Matthew Fox

However we were created by God—and I'll be candid, I wasn't there and I'm not sure it matters how it happened—it remains for me inarguable that we *were* created by God, and that God declared us to be good, and that God loved us then and loves us still. These are basics with which we have to work. And they're good basics, I think.

The Spirit of God of which Jesus spoke in Luke 4 is the same one that leads us, and empowers us to be called children of God. We are adopted to "sonship."

Now, before we go any further, we need to unpack this a little.

Of course this includes everyone, and normally I would use inclusive language. However, in this particular instance there is a point to using the word "sonship" because, at the time this letter was written to the Romans, being a son carried benefits that did not belong to others. Rightly or wrongly, that was the reality of the day.

The Greek word used here for "sonship" means achieving "the full legal standing of an adopted male heir in Roman culture." Kind of like when turning 18 (or whatever is the legal age of majority in your community). You get certain rights and responsibilities. You have arrived.

The point is not gender. Rather, Paul is saying "God's spirit adopts you—all of you, everyone of you, no matter who you are—into full relationship with God. Men, women, slave, free, young, old, black, white, pink, green, straight, gay, married, single—everybody. No strings attached. You all have the benefits that might have formerly only belonged to a few."

This is complete inclusion and acceptance.

Of everyone.

That's why we are also invited to call God "Abba." Again, while this is technically a masculine term, the point here is not the "masculine-ness" of it, but the implied intimacy. Jesus

spoke Aramaic, and probably used the word Abba when referring to God, which is why Paul has used it here. It is best
translated "Papa."

In short, through the work of God's spirit, we not only
have full inheritance rights, but our relationship with God has
no distance—we don't call God "Sir" or "Madam," but "Dad"
or "Mama."

No wonder all creation is so excited! J.B. Phillips translated
verse 19, "The whole creation is on tiptoe to see the wonderful
sight of the [children] of God coming into their own."[9]

While the *via creativa* leads us into the *via transformativa*, it
also contains a bit of a return to the *via positiva*, for it involves
a new appreciation for creation—of which, as we have seen,
we are an intrinsic and blessed part. We see, touch, smell,
taste, and hear it anew.

Becoming new creation does not mean that the old is "bad"
but rather has become "new and improved."

Released from its "bondage to decay" (Romans 8:21) at the
hands of the powers of the world, creation returns to its glori-
ous flower as the wondrous, precious, sacred thing that God
fashioned and intended, and loved from the beginning. We,
God's children, are a part of that and stewards of that.

What will we do?

That is the *via transformativa*.

Week Four:
via transformativa

God has entered in
over and over again;
I transform, transcend.

December 18

Matthew 1:1-17, THE MESSAGE

¹The family tree of Jesus Christ, David's son, Abraham's son:
²Abraham had Isaac,
    Isaac had Jacob,
    Jacob had Judah and his brothers,
³Judah had Perez and Zerah (the mother was Tamar),
    Perez had Hezron,
    Hezron had Aram,
⁴Aram had Amminadab,
    Amminadab had Nahshon,
    Nahshon had Salmon,
⁵Salmon had Boaz (his mother was Rahab),
    Boaz had Obed (Ruth was the mother),
    Obed had Jesse,
⁶Jesse had David,
    and David became king.
David had Solomon (Uriah's wife was the mother),
⁷Solomon had Rehoboam,
    Rehoboam had Abijah,
    Abijah had Asa,
⁸Asa had Jehoshaphat,
    Jehoshaphat had Joram,
    Joram had Uzziah,
⁹Uzziah had Jotham,
    Jotham had Ahaz,
    Ahaz had Hezekiah,
¹⁰Hezekiah had Manasseh,
    Manasseh had Amon,
    Amon had Josiah,

¹¹Josiah had Jehoiachin and his brothers,
   and then the people were taken into the
   Babylonian exile.
¹²When the Babylonian exile ended,
   Jehoiachin had Shealtiel,
   Shealtiel had Zerubbabel,
¹³Zerubbabel had Abiud,
   Abiud had Eliakim,
   Eliakim had Azor,
¹⁴Azor had Zadok,
   Zadok had Achim,
   Achim had Eliud,
¹⁵Eliud had Eleazar,
   Eleazar had Matthan,
   Matthan had Jacob,
¹⁶Jacob had Joseph, Mary's husband,
   the Mary who gave birth to Jesus,
   the Jesus who was called Christ.
¹⁷There were fourteen generations from Abraham to
David,
   another fourteen from David to the Babylonian exile,
   and yet another fourteen from the Babylonian exile to
Christ.

Jesus, God's Chosen, has an impressive pedigree.
   —*Matthew 1:1,* Good as New

When I was quite young, I thought I would read the New Testament from cover to cover, so I started with Matthew, chapter 1. Not exactly the most reader-friendly bit of text in the Bible!

You might wonder at a glance, "what's the point?" Is it really that vital to list all of these people?

Well, yes.

The historical accuracy of the piece is not too crucial—and thus, there isn't any great value in memorizing the thing (hopefully no Sunday School teacher ever actually made anyone do that). But the central fact of the genealogy's existence is vital to understanding that the presence of God's anointed—Messiah in Hebrew, Christ in Greek—in the person of Jesus of Nazareth was quite intentional.

Matthew's genealogy is no less than "a cosmic Christ statement putting Jesus' birth in the context of the history of the universe."[10]

The author of this gospel wants us to understand Jesus as a pivotal point of history, as a part of God's cosmic intention. Not so much the one *predicted* by the prophets, but the one who fulfilled the prophetic vision.

Just as there are patterns to the cosmos—rhythms in which the world and the planets revolve, rhythms to the seasons and turnings of our lives—so Jesus is a part of the cosmic rhythm. Hence, the patterns of 14 that crop up in the genealogy. They may not be historically accurate, but they are spiritually accurate: Jesus is part of that cosmic rhythm, part of a spiritual rhythm, a pattern of the universe that is greater than our comprehension. Jesus is the wondrous confluence of God's divine Word made flesh.

The gospel of John put it in exactly those words, but Matthew puts it in this more Hebrew fashion—a genealogy, a timeline, with its rather typical and traditional patterns.

And yet … there is something profoundly non-traditional about this genealogy, too, which makes it a brilliant starting point for the *via transformativa*.

One might expect, in the genealogy or pedigree of Jesus the Jewish Messiah, a long list of Jewish men; after all, that's how things were done in those days. You listed the fathers, and the grandfathers, and the great-grandfathers, and so on down the line.

But this one is quite different.

There are women.

And there are non-Jews.

And there are what one might call "skeletons in the closet."

We have David: the majestic ruler who united the kingdoms of Israel and Judah. The great composer of so many psalms. The fearless youth who defeated the tyrant Goliath. The one who played his harp to sooth King Saul's raging mood swings.

David who loved so many women, and loved Jonathan more than any woman. David who went to war against Saul, and yet spared Saul's life when David could easily have killed him.

David who abused his power to take advantage of Bathsheba and, when he found she was pregnant, hatched a plot to murder her husband Uriah.

Yes, *that* David.

And it is that particular story from David's life that Matthew recalls for us in Jesus' family tree.

There is Ruth, a woman of amazing faith and compassion, who gives up what seems to be any hope of a happy life for herself in order to care for Naomi. Ruth who is a Moabite, a tribe of people considered among the lowest of the low. Now here she is, in the family tree of the Jewish Messiah.

Rahab, a prostitute who assists the ones sent ahead to scout out the promised land.

You get the idea.

A ragtag mix of outsiders and strangers, people who might not, at first glance, be on the top of the list to be invited to dinner. And that is precisely the point. Because these are the kinds of people that Jesus *would* invite to dinner.

These are the very kinds of people that Jesus dines with, and gathers around him, and tells stories to, and spends time with.

These are the very people to whom, Jesus says, the realm of God belongs.

This is a new world, into which Jesus is born.

This is a new world *because* Jesus is born into it.

This is a new world because you and I are in it: called and invited and equipped by God to transform it.

In this fourth path of the spiritual journey, we are transformed and transforming. There are all sorts of wonderful ways to do this. For us who are Christian, we find ourselves especially transformed by encounter with Jesus the Christ, the Messiah, the child of Mary and Joseph, descendant of Ruth and David and Tamar and Judah and Bathsheba and Solomon and all of those unfamiliar people too, from Amminadab to Zerubbabel.

December 19

Luke 1:46-55, THE MESSAGE

⁴⁶And Mary said,
   I'm bursting with God-news;
⁴⁷I'm dancing the song of my Savior God.
⁴⁸God took one good look at me, and look what happened—
   I'm the most fortunate woman on earth!
⁴⁹What God has done for me will never be forgotten,
   the God whose very name is holy, set apart from all others.
⁵⁰His mercy flows in wave after wave
   on those who are in awe before him.
⁵¹He bared his arm and showed his strength,
   scattered the bluffing braggarts.
⁵²He knocked tyrants off their high horses,
   pulled victims out of the mud.
⁵³The starving poor sat down to a banquet;
   the callous rich were left out in the cold.
⁵⁴He embraced his chosen child, Israel;
   he remembered and piled on the mercies, piled them high.
⁵⁵It's exactly what he promised,
   beginning with Abraham and right up to now.

Now, throughout the townships ringing,
hear the black Madonna cry,
songs of hope and freedom singing,
poor and humble lifted high.

> *Here the Spirit finds a womb*
> *for the breaker of the tomb!*
> *—Michael Forster*

The Bible is full of stories of God calling prophets, and their responses. In most cases, the prophets are reluctant: Moses claims to be a nobody. Isaiah says "I am a person of unclean lips." Jeremiah claims to be too young.

Yet the prophet Mary not only says "let it be, according to your word" (or, "I'm ready to serve" in *The Message)* but bursts into song, proclaiming the goodness of God.

We tend not to think of Mary as a prophet. History (well, the church at least) has sought to recall only her virginity, as if that were her primary feature. Ironically, that aspect of Mary's life is somewhat incidental, a piece of the story presented in the gospels to indicate Jesus' divine paternity, not to imply Mary's "purity."

Beyond that, other references to Mary—this song known as the Magnificat, her challenge to Jesus during the wedding at Cana, and her appearance at a gathering of disciples in the early church, just to name a few—show her as being strong and significant.

God has chosen a young, seemingly unimportant teenager to be the mother of the Messiah, and she recognizes the importance of this event with amazing words. We are reminded of the surprise of God's choices.

And, we are challenged by Mary's proclamation.

Notice that she does not say "these things will happen some day" but that they *have* happened. God *has* done these things.

In the anticipated birth of Jesus, God has set in motion astonishing events. The justice spoken of by prophets of previous generations has come to pass.

Mary's moment of breakthrough—*via creativa*—occurred when the angel Gabriel spoke to her. But she recognized it as a moment of *via transformativa* when she said "yes" and declared what God had done, was doing, and would do.

Having grown up Protestant, I never really knew Mary at all. She "belonged" to the Roman Catholics, it seemed, and was an odd mystery. We had a passing acquaintance through Christmas cards and the occasional bit of stained glass or a classical painting, but that was it. I didn't actually meet Mary properly until I was in seminary, through the prophetic words of her song.

And that's a little strange, too, because I had sung the song before—literally sung it, chanted it, as part of the service of evening prayer in the Anglican tradition. But the words never clicked back then; they seemed somehow trapped in history and didn't have any real power.

Robert McAfee Brown recounts the story of a Bible study in South America in the 1970's. The people were exploring the Magnificat, and contrasting these words with images of Mary from pictures and statues they had seen in churches. They noticed the differences between the docile, crowned "queen of heaven" image the church portrayed, and the Mary of the Magnificat. "It sounds as though Mary would look just like me!" one woman said. "My feet are dirty, my hat is old, my hands are rough, and my clothes are torn."[11]

It is time to reclaim Mary, and note who she is. We must not leave her in the stable, simply as the gentle mother, invariably clad in blue, who birthed baby Jesus and held him close. For while she is indeed that, she is much, much more.

Mary is the one who proclaimed the prophetic actions of God that began with the announcement of Christ's birth, and the transformation of our world that was about to occur.

Mary is the one who dared to sing out that the world would never be the same again because of the birth of Jesus.

Hail Mary: prophet of Nazareth.

December 20

Luke 1:46-55, NRSV

46And Mary said, "My soul magnifies the Lord,
47and my spirit rejoices in God my Savior,
48for he has looked with favor on the lowliness
   of his servant.

   Surely, from now on all generations will call me
blessed;
49for the Mighty One has done great things for me,
   and holy is his name.
50His mercy is for those who fear him
   from generation to generation.
51He has shown strength with his arm;
   he has scattered the proud in the thoughts of their
hearts.
52He has brought down the powerful from their thrones,
   and lifted up the lowly;
53he has filled the hungry with good things,
   and sent the rich away empty.
54He has helped his servant Israel,
   in remembrance of his mercy,
55according to the promise he made to our ancestors,
   to Abraham and to his descendants forever."

There is loveliness in the Magnificat, but in that loveliness there is
dynamite.
—William Barclay.

God's mercy is on those who are in awe (a better translation than fear) of God, who are aware of the awesome power of God to transform the world.

God's mercy is upon those who recognize that in Jesus Christ, these great things have come to pass. God has set in motion the dreams of the prophets.

God's mercy.

Mary mentions it twice in her song.

It is for people of all time, who notice God.

And in verse 54, Mary proclaims that God helps the people because God remembers his mercy, reconnecting with an essential, divine nature.

Neil Douglas-Klotz, in his pioneering work of trying to reconstruct the Aramaic words of Jesus and render them directly into English, reminds us that the Hebrew word for mercy comes from the same root as the word for womb, and is in turn connected with compassion.

God's mercy, God's compassion, brings about a new world.

When that mercy dwells within us, *we* bring about a new world.

Thus, when the Christ is born in us, the world is transformed. Or, as Douglas-Klotz puts it, "a new self is born when the various members of a community, whether inner or outer, change and come together in a new relationship."[12]

This is what Mary sings—that God invites us, together, to birth the new transformed world.

As Mary gave birth to Jesus the Christ, so we can continue, as the body of Christ, to give birth to the newness that Jesus brought into the world.

Each gesture of loving kindness, each act of justice, each moment of transformation, is a birthing of the Christ.

Each lifting up of the lowly, each scattering of the proud, is a birthing of the Christ.

Mary sings of the restoration of balance, harmony, original blessing to the universe.

Now, this was not completely new. Mary (if these are in fact her own words; most scholars suggest that Luke probably exercised a fair bit of editorial license here) may well have been recalling the song of Hannah from 1 Samuel 2:1-10. Hannah was a barren woman who had prayed over and over again for a child. Eventually, she became pregnant and gave birth to a son, the prophet Samuel. Believing this to be God's answer to her prayer, she dedicated the child to serve in the Temple, and sang a song of praise to God with words that get echoed in the Magnificat.

Yet there is also a big difference. As Rev. Sandra Olwine, a United Methodist minister working in the Middle East, comments, Mary transforms Hannah's song from something personal to being "about a broader, social, more political kind of revolution. It is the tying of both spiritual and personal salvation with a sense of liberation that is both social and economic. It is about sort of turning the tables, it is about a God who is about turning the tables, and setting those who are oppressed, who are under the thumb and foot of others, free."[13]

Attending seminary in the 1980's, I became aware of places where the Magnificat was banned from public reading, considered to be subversive, even "communist propaganda" at one point. I could swear I actually heard Mary quietly snickering over that.

Governments only ban things when they feel threatened. It's intriguing to think of dictators feeling threatened by a dozen verses ostensibly uttered by a pregnant, teenage peasant some 2,000 years ago.

Yet they are indeed subversive, for in these prophetic words we hear a proclamation of nothing less than the power of God to transform the world, through human actions.

Beauty and power indeed.

December 21

Matthew 1:18-25, THE MESSAGE

[18]The birth of Jesus took place like this. His mother, Mary, was engaged to be married to Joseph. Before they came to the marriage bed, Joseph discovered she was pregnant. (It was by the Holy Spirit, but he didn't know that.) [19]Joseph, chagrined but noble, determined to take care of things quietly so Mary would not be disgraced.

[20]While he was trying to figure a way out, he had a dream. God's angel spoke in the dream: "Joseph, son of David, don't hesitate to get married. Mary's pregnancy is Spirit-conceived. God's Holy Spirit has made her pregnant. [21]She will bring a son to birth, and when she does, you, Joseph, will name him Jesus—'God saves'—because he will save his people from their sins." [22]This would bring the prophet's embryonic sermon to full term:

[23]Watch for this—a virgin will get pregnant and bear a son;

They will name him Emmanuel (Hebrew for "God is with us").

[24]Then Joseph woke up. He did exactly what God's angel commanded in the dream: He married Mary. [25]But he did not consummate the marriage until she had the baby. He named the baby Jesus.

A baby is God's opinion that the world should go on.
—Carl Sandburg

I first encountered this story in Sunday School in the King James Version, and we boys would all snicker at the various euphemisms that cropped up in the ancient text.

In what was hardly a more innocent time (it just seemed that way) we found something quite titillating about this story of Joseph discovering that the woman to whom he was engaged was pregnant, and that he was not the father. In particular, we all thought there was something outrageously funny about the use of the verb "know" with reference to sex in verse 25: "And he knew her not till she had brought forth her firstborn son …"

Today, as I read this story (and *not* in the King James Version) I am struck by the nature of this person called Joseph, and what he teaches us about life in the new era being ushered in by the child about to be born.

We could get hung up on technical questions about Mary's virginity and the conception of Jesus, and miss the more important story here, which has to do with Joseph's actions.

Joseph, we are told, is a "righteous man"—the translation above uses the word "noble." As a righteous man, he presumably obeys the Jewish law, which is quite clearly spelled out in the Bible.

When the story begins, Joseph is presented with an extremely difficult dilemma. His fiancée appears to have committed adultery. How else is he expected to understand her pregnancy, since he knows that he hasn't slept with her?

Furthermore, the law is very clear on how to respond. Deuteronomy 22:20-21 states that the men of the town are to stone Mary to death.

As a righteous man, Joseph ought to uphold the law. It's what would be expected. It was the "right" thing to do.

Except …

Except that Joseph decides to redefine what it means to be righteous.

Joseph decides that, because he is righteous, he will defy the law. He chooses to divorce Mary privately (without going into all the technicalities of betrothal and marriage law in those days, suffice it to say that, even though they weren't married the way we would understand it, breaking the engagement still required a formal divorce.)

Joseph decided that he could not condone killing someone, and sought to send Mary away to safety, despite the fact that he was blatantly going against biblical law. Despite the fact that he was contradicting what he had been taught to believe was God's law.

We can only guess as to why Joseph did this, but I have a hunch that Joseph knew that a law which required stoning a woman to death for being pregnant would *not* be the will of God.

It is after making this decision that Joseph learns the real story of Mary's pregnancy. And then he makes another decision: to marry her and live with her.

So now, after breaking the law, he goes one step further and risks public shame and ridicule by marrying a woman who is going to have a child that everyone knows is not his.

Let's be honest: surely God could have sent the Christ to be born in any one of a number of different ways. At the very least, a conventional, married couple could have been chosen as the parents.

But Matthew gives us this story. A story of someone named Joseph who is faced with a huge moral dilemma.

Having been taught to believe that the torah, God's law, was the way of life, Joseph was now feeling called to reject a part of it in the name of compassion. It can't have been easy.

Why do we have this story?

Perhaps, like Luke's story of Mary's song, Matthew is showing us the new era that the Christ is bringing.

When rules conflict with God's way of compassion, we are called to follow the way of compassion, even when it means changing our worldview, even when it means risking shame and ridicule, even when it means rejecting parts of scripture.

Jesus teaches and models this over and over again. Yet, even before Jesus, Joseph gives a foretaste of what is to come.

This is the new righteousness, Joseph tells us: compassion.

December 22

Matthew 1:1 8-2 5, NRSV

[18]Now the birth of Jesus the Messiah took place in this way. When his mother Mary had been engaged to Joseph, but before they lived together, she was found to be with child from the Holy Spirit. [19]Her husband Joseph, being a righteous man and unwilling to expose her to public disgrace, planned to dismiss her quietly. [20]But just when he had resolved to do this, an angel of the Lord appeared to him in a dream and said, "Joseph, son of David, do not be afraid to take Mary as your wife, for the child conceived in her is from the Holy Spirit. [21]She will bear a son, and you are to name him Jesus, for he will save his people from their sins." [22]All this took place to fulfill what had been spoken by the Lord through the prophet: [23]"Look, the virgin shall conceive and bear a son, and they shall name him Emmanuel," which means, "God is with us."

[24]When Joseph awoke from sleep, he did as the angel of the Lord commanded him; he took her as his wife, [25] but had no marital relations with her until she had borne a son; and he named him Jesus.

Justice and power must be brought together, so that whatever is just may be powerful, and whatever is powerful may be just.
—Blaise Pascal

One of the things that always struck me as odd in Matthew's version of the Christmas story is the business of Jesus' name.

In a dream, an angel tells Joseph to name the child Jesus.

Then Matthew says that this fulfills the prophecy that says a young woman will have a child called Emmanuel.

So Mary has a child, and they name him Jesus.

I don't quibble with the names—they are both excellent, and have much to say about this incarnation of the Christ, as I'll explore below.

It just seems strange that Matthew provides, as explanation of the name Jesus, the prophecy about the name Emmanuel.

I've come to the conclusion that Matthew could have used a good editor.

Matthew loves a good text to support the whole story of the birth of Jesus/Emmanuel. In fact, Matthew quotes the Hebrew scriptures five times in the first two chapters of the gospel (not counting all of the references in the genealogy).

The bottom line, however, is that we are left with two rather good names. One—Jesus—we use the vast majority of the time. The other—Emmanuel (sometimes spelled Immanuel)—tends to get confined to Advent and Christmas carols. But it's a great name.

It's made up of three Hebrew words: *im* (with) + *manu* (us) + *el* (God).

The word for God used here is a form of the name used in Genesis 1, which is the story of God creating in a very orderly fashion. This is *via transformativa,* this presence of the God who brings order out of chaos, now coming into our world in a new and unique way to make sense out of life. Once again, God seeks to bring order out of chaos—this time by living among us, as one of us.

God-with-us.

God is always with us, so in one sense, the birth of Jesus was nothing new.

On the other hand, it was also something wonderfully new, excitingly new, dynamically new.

God with us in a uniquely human form.

God's word made flesh, as John describes it.

God's very presence, God's very essence (words are so inadequate when speaking of the Divine!) walking, talking, *being* in our midst: touchable, approachable, laughing and questioning and blessing and healing.

This is Emmanuel in the purest form. And this is what Matthew tries to tell us is happening in this child born to Joseph and Mary.

Matthew, who knew well the Hebrew scriptures, is not necessarily telling us that the prophet Isaiah predicted Jesus, but rather saying, "you know, Isaiah talked about God being present with us in a unique and amazing way. Well, folks, that happened. It happened in Jesus. And here's how …"

Transformation happened in the person of Emmanuel.

And transformation happened in Jesus.

The name "Jesus" is an English rendering of the German spelling of the Greek version of the Hebrew name that usually gets written "Joshua."

Confusing, isn't it?

It's just that, if Jesus were here today and someone said the name "Jesus" he wouldn't answer because, well, that was never the way his name was pronounced. It sounded something like Yeshua, with the accent on the "shu" syllable.

But the sound is not the issue—it's the meaning that really matters.

Jesus/Joshua/Yeshua means "God saves."

Interestingly, this uses a different Hebrew name for God. Emmanuel used "Elohim" but Jesus uses the name Yahweh. In the creation stories, this name is used in the Genesis 2 story, the one where God is more down to earth, breathing into mud figures, and chatting with the creation.

This God, in the person of Jesus of Nazareth, saves.

But what does "salvation" mean? It's one of those religious jargon words that can so often get misconstrued. Frequently it gets tossed around without much thought. People talk about being "saved" as if it somehow puts them in a different category than others—sort of an "I'm saved and you're not" kind of mentality.

Or, we may have the sense that we are saved *from* something, as if Jesus has come to rescue us.

Perhaps there is a certain amount of truth to that. I know that the presence of Jesus Christ in my life helps keep me from becoming obsessed with myself. I know that being a part of Christian community has moved me away from a self-serving life.

But as I grow increasingly on my spiritual journey, and especially in the context of the *via transformativa*, I more and more have come to realize that Jesus saves me not *from* anything, but *to* something.

Because the word that usually gets translated "save" in the Bible is a word that in other contexts means "wholeness."

Jesus does not "save us from" things so much as Jesus restores us to wholeness.

Jesus "saves the people" by restoring in us the presence of the divine breath that has been forgotten, that we have denied, that the world has tried to snuff out.

Salvation means returning to the wholeness that our Creator has intended for us all along, that we have neglected, that we have moved away from.

We do not need to be rescued *from* anything nearly so much as we need to be restored *to* something.

In Emmanuel we experience the unique, transforming presence of God.

In Jesus, we are transformed by a return to our divinely-ordained wholeness.

Jesus.

Emmanuel.

The Savior with us.

December 23

1 John 4: 7-2 1, NRSV

[7]Beloved, let us love one another, because love is from God; everyone who loves is born of God and knows God. [8]Whoever does not love does not know God, for God is love. [9]God's love was revealed among us in this way: God sent his only Son into the world so that we might live through him. [10]In this is love, not that we loved God but that he loved us and sent his Son to be the atoning sacrifice for our sins. [11]Beloved, since God loved us so much, we also ought to love one another. [12]No one has ever seen God; if we love one another, God lives in us, and his love is perfected in us. [13]By this we know that we abide in him and he in us, because he has given us of his Spirit.

[14]And we have seen and do testify that the Father has sent his Son as the Savior of the world. [15]God abides in those who confess that Jesus is the Son of God, and they abide in God.

[16]So we have known and believe the love that God has for us. God is love, and those who abide in love abide in God, and God abides in them.

[17]Love has been perfected among us in this: that we may have boldness on the day of judgment, because as he is, so are we in this world. [18]There is no fear in love, but perfect love casts out fear; for fear has to do with punishment, and whoever fears has not reached perfection in love. [19]We love because he first loved us. [20]Those who say, "I love God," and hate their brothers or sisters, are liars; for those who do not love a brother or sister whom they have seen, cannot love God whom they have not seen. [21]The commandment we have from him is this:

those who love God must love their brothers and sisters also.

> *You may call God love, you may call God goodness. But the best name for God is compassion.*
> —*Meister Eckhart*

People speak about 12-step recovery being a program of "attraction, rather than promotion." In other words, one does not go around saying, "Hi, I'm a recovering alcoholic because of Alcoholics Anonymous." Rather, by living a clean and sober life, others might wonder what has caused the transformation, and want to learn more about it.

This passage sort of says the same thing.

If people see that I am transformed by experiencing the love of God, and living it, they will want to know what it is that has transformed me, and will want perhaps to make acquaintance with the entity that has worked transformation within me. And thus, in turn, the transformation continues, rippling outwards.

The thing is love.

God's love.

We are called to be love, to embody the love of God. To radiate it, to live it.

And we are called to do it, to share it in acts of compassion. Verse 20 minces no words: "Those who say 'I love God,' and hate their brothers or sisters, are liars."

Yet, I have to wonder if the word "must" in verse 21 really is a commandment, or a description of reality.

Those who love God cannot help but love one another; it is the natural outpouring of being filled with God's love. As surely as night follows day and day follows night, those who love God love one another, for God is love. It's the way it works.

And as we are consumed with love for God, overwhelmed by God's love, madly and passionately *in love* with God, we are also madly and passionately in love with the universe, with God's creation. With every rock, tree, kangaroo, child, woman, man, river, mountain, and skyscraper that is an integral and vital part of the universe.

We speak of "loving" God, but we need to move a step beyond that to being "in love" with God. To being romantically involved with God. Intimately involved.

Living as we do in a world where the governing principle seems to be "get what you can to make yourself happy" we need the reminder that our response to being loved by God is to love God back. And we do that by loving God's creation, God's creatures.

Too often we can be tempted to shop around for any manner of anything, until we find the thing that tickles our fancy, whether it's materially, romantically, or spiritually.

The Creator says to us: *I am it. I am the only. However you wish to call me, to understand me, to envision me, there is one creation, and one Creator.*

I love you.

Love me back, by loving one another.

Just as we do not see the wind, but see what it does, in the same way, we do not see the love of God, except when it is made real, in lives transformed, and in acts of compassion.

December 24

1 John 4:16b-21, NRSV

[16b]God is love, and those who abide in love abide in God, and God abides in them.

[17]Love has been perfected among us in this: that we may have boldness on the day of judgment, because as he is, so are we in this world. [18]There is no fear in love, but perfect love casts out fear; for fear has to do with punishment, and whoever fears has not reached perfection in love. [19]We love because he first loved us. [20]Those who say, "I love God," and hate their brothers or sisters, are liars; for those who do not love a brother or sister whom they have seen, cannot love God whom they have not seen. [21]The commandment we have from him is this: those who love God must love their brothers and sisters also.

> *I need more grace than I thought.*
> *—Rumi*

We live in a climate of fear. Constantly, the government and the media encourage us to be afraid: of nature, of one another, of the economy.

How welcome is the angelic message once again, "Do not fear, for I bring you tidings of great joy for all people."

All people.

Great joy.

Do not fear.

There is no fear in love, but perfect love casts out fear.

That is good news, good news that the world needs to hear.

Fear has to do with punishment, and whoever fears has not reached perfection in love.

Now, I don't think that means we have to figure out the perfect way to love others (although that would be an admirable goal) but rather to experience the love of God. To know that we are loved. Unconditionally. No strings attached. The grace thing.

Knowing we are loved by God—knowing that we are an original blessing—empowers us to live without fear.

This in turn affects how we live and how we respond to others.

For example, the US government has a color-coded system for instilling fear in the populace. It's some kind of terrorism alert system. I honestly don't understand what it is actually based on, but I do know that whenever I am in an airport a recorded voice frequently tells me that "the Department of Homeland Security has decreed the terrorism alert level to be turquoise" or some other color.

I don't know if that is supposed to scare me, or make me feel more secure.

But frankly it does neither. Instead it spurs me into action. I go on rainbow alert.

To heck with trying to figure out the colors that the government wants me to know, I go with the colors of God's promise, the colors of hope, the colors of inclusion.

Rainbow alert.

Instead of letting a color tell me whom to fear, I let it be a reminder that, as a child of God, I have an obligation—a joyous obligation—to be a little more friendly, a little more welcoming.

I have the opportunity to counter fear and terrorism and hatred and discord by being a little more loving toward others. I try to smile more. I try to be friendlier and more forgiving.

Instead of being afraid of other people, I remember that the Bible calls us to love them.

I recall that, even in infancy, Jesus welcomed strangers—shepherds, and magi—modeling for us that we are to open our arms and our hearts as we seek to love our brothers and sisters, not close our eyes to the beautiful people all around us.

Love *has* been perfected in us.

This is the message of Isaiah 9 that is so often read on Christmas Eve:

> [2]The people who walked in darkness have seen a great light; those who lived in a land of deep darkness—on them light has shined.
> [6]For a child has been born for us, a son given to us; authority rests upon his shoulders; and he is named Wonderful Counselor, Mighty God, Everlasting Father, Prince of Peace.
> [7]His authority shall grow continually, and there shall be endless peace for the throne of David and his kingdom. He will establish and uphold it with justice and with righteousness from this time onward and forevermore. The zeal of the LORD of hosts will do this. *(NRSV)*

It is the message we celebrate as Advent gives way to Christmas. The light of the primal flaring forth, the light of God that shines in the darkness, the light that happened when God said "let there be ..." shines now. It will *not* go away.

We need not fear.

May the world go on rainbow alert.

Postlude: to You Is Born this Day

Luke 2: 1-2 0, *NRSV*

[1]In those days a decree went out from Emperor Augustus that all the world should be registered. [2]This was the first registration and was taken while Quirinius was governor of Syria.

[3]All went to their own towns to be registered. [4]Joseph also went from the town of Nazareth in Galilee to Judea, to the city of David called Bethlehem, because he was descended from the house and family of David. [5]He went to be registered with Mary, to whom he was engaged and who was expecting a child. [6]While they were there, the time came for her to deliver her child.

[7]And she gave birth to her firstborn son and wrapped him in bands of cloth, and laid him in a manger, because there was no place for them in the inn.

[8]In that region there were shepherds living in the fields, keeping watch over their flock by night. [9]Then an angel of the Lord stood before them, and the glory of the Lord shone around them, and they were terrified. [10]But the angel said to them, "Do not be afraid; for see—I am bringing you good news of great joy for all the people: [11]to you is born this day in the city of David a Savior, who is the Messiah, the Lord. [12]This will be a sign for

you: you will find a child wrapped in bands of cloth and lying in a manger."

[13]And suddenly there was with the angel a multitude of the heavenly host, praising God and saying, [14]"Glory to God in the highest heaven, and on earth peace among those whom he favors!"

[15]When the angels had left them and gone into heaven, the shepherds said to one another, "Let us go now to Bethlehem and see this thing that has taken place, which the Lord has made known to us." [16]So they went with haste and found Mary and Joseph, and the child lying in the manger. [17]When they saw this, they made known what had been told them about this child; [18]and all who heard it were amazed at what the shepherds told them. [19]But Mary treasured all these words and pondered them in her heart. [20]The shepherds returned, glorifying and praising God for all they had heard and seen, as it had been told them.

And so this is Christmas, and what have you done?
Another year over, a new one just begun.
—Yoko Ono and John Lennon

Addressing the General Council of the United Church of Canada in 1997, Archbishop Desmond Tutu invited people to imagine being in Bethlehem the night Jesus was born.

"You're walking past the stable, and you see a baby lying in a manger. Casually you say to the mother, 'who is that?' And she says, 'Oh, that's God.'

"That frail, little thing, lying in a manger? Oh God, how can you have such low standards?"[14]

Yet God's standards are not low, and I think that was the Archbishop's point.

God's standards are just right.

God comes to dwell among us in a unique way, in a mysterious way. Huge volumes are written trying to define the nature of how Jesus is both fully divine and fully human. But on Christmas Day, I don't know that it matters so much as simply basking in the reality of the simple truth: to us is born this day a Savior, the Messiah, the Sovereign one, Jesus, the Christ.

No words are adequate to sum up the good news the angels sought to convey to the shepherds. It took glory filling the heavens, and the shivering awe and amazement of experiencing with all the sense the awareness of God's overwhelming presence.

This is good news, of great joy, to all people.

There's that word "good," just like at the beginning of creation.

And great joy—coupled with the announcement "do not fear." The presence of God in our midst is indeed a joyous thing, not something to cause us to run and hide. God here among us is affirmation of our original blessing; the birth of Jesus is the ultimate divine hug.

To all people.

The angelic message is not reserved for some. As Mary gave the world advance notice, as Matthew's genealogy alerts us, the arrival of Jesus on the world stage is a reminder that God's love is for all. God's promise is for all. *God* is for all.

What's left now is for us to respond to this good news.

We can take our cue from the shepherds, who did two things. They went to see, and then they went out to celebrate.

Go and see the Christ. Go and encounter Christ. That need not involve actually *going* anywhere, but simply allowing yourself to become aware: aware of the presence of Christ in your world, in your life. Open yourself—each and every one of your senses—to this wonderful and unique form of God's presence in our world, Jesus the Christ, the Messiah, the child of God.

Do it often. Repeatedly. Let it be a pattern.

Allow yourself to be transformed by the simple awareness that God loves you—us—all of us—the whole world, so very much that God has never abandoned us, and in fact chose to live among us in Jesus of Nazareth to prove without a shadow of a doubt that God's love was never-ending.

Then go … and celebrate.

Celebrate that love like you celebrate nothing else. With joy, with zeal, with a passion for God's justice, with a hope that is limitless.

That doesn't mean a smile all the time, but the deeper joy, the richer joy, the joy that "magnifies God" as Mary said. The joy that issues forth in wanting the best for all of God's people because God has done the best for you.

I'm convinced that, if we are open to the reality of Christmas, we cannot help but be changed.

If we're just looking for some mythical happiness, like the kind that appears in some ideal Norman Rockwell painting, or a made-for-TV movie (which *might* happen), we'll be ultimately disappointed. Because that stuff, while nice, isn't very ultimate.

But if we are looking for the amazing transformation that God has offered, has promised, has in store for us, then look out world—it's going to be pretty awesome!

We may know this story, but it can still surprise us. Maybe not the story itself, but the truth of it—the amazement of it, the reality that God enters our daily living.

God invites us up a mountain to learn the ways of peace.

God brings down the mighty and lifts up the lowly.

God shines a light in the depths of the world's night, and defies the world to put it out. And nothing has yet defeated it, not even diminished it.

So … celebrate Christmas. This day. Every day.

Think of Ebenezer Scrooge, and his spiritual journey. We meet him in the midst of his *via negativa*, but the ghost of Christmas past shows us glimpses of a happier time *(positiva)*. All three spirits conspire in the breakthrough *(creativa)* that results in Scrooge's transformation, enabling him to declare "I will keep Christmas every day of the year."

May the same be said of us.

Blessed be.

Appendix:
The Magi and the
Spiritual Journey: a brief
introduction to Creation
Spirituality

Matthew 2:1-12, NRSV

¹In the time of King Herod, after Jesus was born in Bethlehem of Judea, wise men from the East came to Jerusalem, ²asking, "Where is the child who has been born king of the Jews? For we observed his star at its rising, and have come to pay him homage."

³ When King Herod heard this, he was frightened, and all Jerusalem with him; ⁴and calling together all the chief priests and scribes of the people, he inquired of them where the Messiah was to be born. ⁵They told him, "In Bethlehem of Judea; for so it has been written by the prophet:

⁶And you, Bethlehem, in the land of Judah,

are by no means least among the rulers of Judah;

for from you shall come a ruler who is to shepherd my people Israel."

⁷Then Herod secretly called for the wise men and learned from them the exact time when the star had

appeared. [8]Then he sent them to Bethlehem, saying, "Go and search diligently for the child; and when you have found him, bring me word so that I may also go and pay him homage."

[9]When they had heard the king, they set out; and there, ahead of them, went the star that they had seen at its rising, until it stopped over the place where the child was. [10]When they saw that the star had stopped, they were overwhelmed with joy. [11]On entering the house, they saw the child with Mary his mother; and they knelt down and paid him homage. Then, opening their treasure chests, they offered him gifts of gold, frankincense, and myrrh. [12]And having been warned in a dream not to return to Herod, they left for their own country by another road.

The story of the magi's journey to Bethlehem provides an intriguing paradigm for the spiritual journey, especially in terms of the four paths of Creation Spirituality.

Firstly, there is the path of original blessing, what we call the *via positiva*, the wondrous moment where we encounter the divine. The magi see a star, and in that star they experience the presence of God. While they do not seem to know the exact whereabouts or identity of the God that the star represents, they recognize immediately the wondrous nature of the holy one worthy of their pursuit. So it is with us. From the earliest moments of our life journey, we cannot—nor need we—put a name to the divine presence we feel, yet we know that there is an "other" that is out there, and all around, and inside us, too. There is a something that has created us and called us good, and which loves us without question or limit, and thus our desire to follow that something, that source of divine light, becomes our life's pursuit.

Yet just as every picture has its mirror opposite, there is the ***via negativa***. The magi encounter Herod, an exquisite manifestation of jealousy and pride and power and ego. We can deny the presence of such things in our world, and in our lives, but we do so at our own peril. Religious systems that encourage us to ignore these things, to pretend that they don't exist, leave us ill-prepared. On the other hand, those that paint the Herods of the world as frightening bogey-men from which to flee don't help much, either. The magi enter Herod's palace, but they don't enter into his scheming. Their awareness of the star's brightness—its affirmation of their own worth and goodness—seems to empower them. Herod's fear of the light of the star and the divine blessing it represents seems far greater than the false power that he presumes to yield.

Too often, we run in fear from things that are in fact much less powerful than we have been led to believe. If we trust that our loving Creator is eager to accompany us on the spiritual journey, we can dare to embrace the night and find that the dawn shines far brighter. Herod stays at home in fear. The magi journey on.

The breakthrough of a new day is called the ***via creativa***. Shedding the sleaze of Herod's dishonesty (the story goes on to tell us that Herod only wanted to find out where Jesus was so he could kill him), the magi find that the star seems even brighter, and the promise of God's new presence seems that much closer. The strength to continue is all the greater for having dared the darkness—not in having conquered it so much as extracting from it what it can offer (Herod's aides did offer the magi some assistance, after all) and remembering that the awesome power of God is greater than all that can frighten us. How often fear paralyzes and stifles us, and prevents us from seeing the journey through. Yet when we do continue the journey, we find it takes us into the presence of Christ, of God incarnate, the Word made flesh. God pleased to dwell in the midst of the creation.

And the magi's response? They go home by a different road. The circle is completed in the path of transformation, ***via transformativa***. Our encounter with God in Christ transforms us. We go forth to transform our world. We cannot help but go by a different road, to live by a different way. If we allow ourselves to be fully and unconditionally in the presence of the Christ, we are changed.

May we do the same. May we encounter the Christ child. And then go home by a different path.

Sources of quotations

The haiku introducing the four paths (pp. 1, 33, 63, and 89) are by Donald Schmidt.

Prelude: Helen Keller, from www.quotationspage.com/quote/3141.html, retrieved June 29, 2007.

November 27: Cited in Matthew Fox, *Original Blessing* (Santa Fe: Bear and Co., 1983), p. 42.

November 28: Cited in Bruce Sanguin, *Darwin, Divinity, and the Dance of the Cosmos: an Ecological Christianity* (Kelowna, BC: CopperHouse, 2007), p. 45.

November 29: Fred Rogers, *Life's Journeys According to Mr. Rogers—Things to Remember along the Way* (NY: Hyperion, 2005), p. 53.

November 30: Hawksley Workman, *hawksley burns for Isadora* (Toronto: Gutter Press, 2000).

December 1: Daniel A. Helminiak, *The Transcended Christian: Spiritual Lessons for the Twenty-first Century* (New York: Alyson Books, 2007), p. 306.

December 2: Sam Keen, *Hymns to an Unknown God: Awakening the Spirit in Everyday Life* (New York: Bantam, 1994), p. 33.

December 3: Sanguin, *Darwin, Divinity, and the Dance of the Cosmos,* p. 24.

December 4: Matthew Fox, *Meditations with Meister Eckhart* (Santa Fe: Bear and Co., 1983), p. 45.

December 5: Traditional Shaker hymn.

December 6: Rogers, *Life's Journeys,* p. 44.

December 7: Source unknown.

December 8: Source unknown—I have had this quotation rattling around in my head since I first heard it in my teens, and I searched the internet, but could not find its origins.

December 9: Rogers, *Life's Journeys,* p. 17.

December 10: Dom Helder Camara, *A Thousand Reasons for Living,* edited by José de Broucker, translated by Alan Neame (Philadelphia: Fortress Press, 1981), p. 19.

December 11: Leonard Cohen, "Anthem," *Stranger Music* (Toronto: McClelland and Stewart, 1993), p. 373.

December 12: Cited in *Awaken: the Art of Imaginative Preaching*, Pentecost 1 2007, Year C (Inver Grove Hts., MN: Logos Productions, 2007), p. 44.

December 13: From an address made by Archbishop Desmond Tutu at the University of Toronto's Convocation Hall on February 16 2000. Retrieved May 17, 2007, from http://www.trinity.utoronto.ca/Alumni/tutu.htm

December 14: Cited in Paul Hawker, *Soul Quest: a Spiritual Odyssey through 40 Days and 40 Nights of Mountain Solitude* (Kelowna, BC: Northstone, 2006), p. 48.

December 15: Although frequently attributed to Lila Watson (whose name is also spelled Lilla Watson), and while Ms Watson has used the quotation publicly, she prefers not to take credit for coming up with it, claiming that it was born in community. More information about the source of this quotation comes from the blog of the Northland Poster collective, found at http://northlandposter.com/blog/2006/12/18/(accessed May 26, 2007).

December 16: His Holiness the XIV Dalai Lama, *The Four Noble Truths,* translated by Geshe Thupten Jinpa (London: Thorsons, 1997), p. 134–135.

December 17: Fox, *Original Blessing,* p. 204.

December 18: John Henson, *Good as New: a Radical Retelling of the Scriptures* (New York: O Books, 2004), p. 124.

December 19: Michael Forster, "Mary, Blessed Teenage Mother" © 1992 Kevin Mayhew Ltd., in *Hymns Old and New: New Anglican Edition* (London: Kevin Mayhew Ltd., 1996).

December 20: William Barclay, *The Daily Study Bible: The Gospel of Luke* (Toronto: G.R. Welch, 1975), p. 16.

December 21: Carl Sandburg, from http://www.brainy quote.com/quotes/authors/c/carl_sandburg.html, retrieved July 2, 2007.

December 22: Blaise Pascal, from http://www.brainy quote.com/quotes/authors/b/blaise_pascal.html, retrieved July 2, 2007.

December 23: Fox, *Meditations with Meister Eckhart*, p. 111.

December 24: Rumi, "Dissolve of Sugar," in Coleman Barks and John Moyne, trans., *The Essential Rumi* (New York: Harper Collins, 1997), p. 53.

December 25: John Lennon and Yoko Ono, "Happy Xmas(War Is Over)," from the EMI Records album *Shaved Fish* © 1971 by EMI Blackwood Music Inc. o/b/o Lenono Music.

Notes

1. W.J.A. Power, *Once Upon a Time: a Humorous Re-telling of the Genesis Stories* (Nashville: Abingdon 1992), p. 17.

2. Matthew Fox, *Meditations with Meister Eckhart*, (Santa Fe: Bear and Co., 1983), p. 54.

3. Matthew Fox, *Original Blessing*, (Santa Fe: Bear and Co., 1983), p. 163.

4. Fox, *Original Blessing*, pp. 142–143.

5. John Henson, *Good as New: a Radical Retelling of the Scriptures* (New York: O Books, 2004), p. 168.

6. Matthew Fox, *Creation Spirituality: Liberating Gifts for the Peoples of the Earth* (San Francisco: Harper, 1991), p. 21.

7. Fred Rogers, *Life's Journeys According to Mr. Rogers—Things to Remember along the Way* (NY: Hyperion, 2005), p. 88.

8. Fox, *Original Blessing*, p. 187.

9. J.B. Philips, *The New Testament in Modern English,* (London: Geoffrey Bles, 1960).

10. Matthew Fox, *The Coming of the Cosmic Christ* (San Francisco: Harper, 1988), p. 100.

11. Robert McAfee Brown, *Unexpected News: Reading the Bible with Third World Eyes* (Philadelphia: Westminster Press, 1984), p. 87.

12. Neil Douglas-Klotz, *The Hidden Gospel: Decoding the Spiritual Message of the Aramaic Jesus* (Wheaton, IL: Quest Books, 1999), p. 144.

13. From *Adult/Youth Curriculum Video Resource 1999/ 2000—The Whole People of God* (Toronto: UCTV Spirit Connection in consultation with Wood Lake Books, Kelowna, BC © 1999).

14. From *Adult/Youth Curriculum Video Resource 1997/ 98—The Whole People of God* (Toronto: UCTV Spirit Connection in consultation with Wood Lake Books, Kelowna, BC © 1997).

Other books by Donald Schmidt

Emerging Word: a Creation-Spirituality Lectionary

An invitation to wonder, contemplate, and explore the story that the church has told, is telling, and can tell. This one-year lectionary traces the four paths of Creation Spirituality as it provides scripture readings for the Sundays and major festivals of the Christian year, infusing the traditional seasons with new insight and meaning.

iUniverse, 2006. $14.95
ISBN 0-595-39418-3

Bible Wonderings: Familiar Tales Retold
Twenty-four Bible stories receive new treatment, often with a twist. Like turning a kaleidoscope to see new colors fall into place, these stories provide a fresh seeing and hearing of traditional stories. Sometimes challenging, sometimes whimsical, always thought-provoking. A brief study guide makes the book suitable for Bible study groups.
iUniverse, 2006. $14.95
ISBN 0-595-40311-5

About the author

Donald Schmidt has a passion for the Bible, for the church, for the seasons of the liturgical year, for story-telling, and for justice. Somehow they all manage to get woven together in this book.

He grew up in a combined Anglican/United Church of Canada Sunday School in British Columbia, Canada. Early studies in political science at the University of Victoria were followed by degrees in comparative religion and theology from Montreal's McGill University, and a Doctor of Ministry in Creation Spirituality from Wisdom University in 2006.

Donald has served as a minister in Quebec, New York, Vermont, and Hawai'i. In addition to parish ministry, he has written and edited church school curriculum, worship resources, and Bible study materials for over fifteen years. His songs have been recorded and published in Australia, Canada, Chile, New Zealand, and the U.S.

He has taught church history, worship and preaching, and church dynamics at the Henry Opukaha'ia Center for Pacific Theological Studies.

When not working in the church or writing, or knitting, or playing guitar, or traveling with his spouse, or visiting with grandchildren, Donald likes to spend time enjoying the beauty of God's creation.

For more information, visit www.emergingword.com.

978-0-595-44812-8
0-595-44812-7

CPSIA information can be obtained
at www.ICGtesting.com
Printed in the USA
FSOW01n0553240717
36659FS